Autism Parent
Handbook

Start with the End Goal in Mind

Raun Melmed, MD   Wendela Marsh, MA, BCBA, RSD

Foreword by Temple Grandin

AUTISM PARENT HANDBOOK: Start with the End Goal in Mind

All marketing and publishing rights guaranteed to and reserved by:

FUTURE HORIZONS INC.

(800) 489-0727

(817) 277-0727

(817) 277-2270 (fax)

E-mail: info@fhautism.com

www.fhautism.com

ISBN: 9781949177664

For Reya, Charlie, Arlo, Aurelia and Reuben

RDM

For Anne, Siobhan, and Noel

WWM

CONTENTS

FOREWORD
Temple Grandin,
Author of The Way I See It

The Autism Parent Handbook will be especially useful for parents who have newly diagnosed, verbal and nonverbal children, all the way into adulthood. When I was three years old, I was non-verbal, had constant tantrums, and liked to spin things. Today, I am a university professor. At age 2 ½, I had intensive speech therapy and spent many sessions learning turn-taking by playing board games. This helped me learn to control impulsive behavior.

One problem with autism is it is such a broad spectrum. When the children become adults, they range from a computer programmer working in Silicon Valley to an individual who will still need assistance with basic skills, such as dressing. When a child is very little, their symptoms may be severe. Some of these kids may become fully verbal, and others will not. Research shows very clearly that intensive early educational intervention will improve the prognosis. When fully verbal autistic kids are in the early elementary school grades, it is often easy to observe a skill the child excels in. For me, it was art, and my artistic ability was always encouraged. Mother always urged me to draw many different things. Another kid may be good at math; if so, they should be given more challenging math. A third type of child may like words and facts. Academic skills will often be uneven, and there needs to be a lot more emphasis on developing strengths. If a child develops an interest in cars, then use cars to teach math, science, and reading.

Children who remain non-verbal are usually capable of learning lots of skills. There is a tendency to overprotect the child. A non-verbal child may learn to put on their own clothes, but the parents often do it for them. The problem with autism is that the range of abilities is huge. Albert Einstein would be in special education today because he had severely delayed speech. Another child may remain non-verbal but learn to type independently while still having difficulty controlling their movements. Some children also have other severe medical problems in conjunction with autism, such as epileptic seizures. I remember the frustration of not being able to communicate when I was three. This is why it is so important to provide methods for communication.

When your child starts to learn speech, always give them opportunities to use language. Speak slowly and clearly. When I was young and adults talked quickly, it sounded like gibberish. You also need to give the child time to respond. Autistic kids have a slower processing speed, and more time is required for a response. Concentrate on the things your child can learn to do. I especially recommend this book to parents who have a recently diagnosed young child who is non-verbal.

PREFACE
Begin with the End in Mind

What of the Future?

"Prediction is hard, especially when talking about the future."
— *Yogi Berra*

If you're holding this book, chances are you either have learned or suspect that your child has Autism Spectrum Disorder (ASD). You are looking at a toddler or preschooler, or whatever age your child is right now, and the future feels insurmountable. It may be frightening to ponder what is in store for this little one. But, just for a moment, let us step into a time machine and visualize your fondest wishes and hopes for your child's future. Let us begin now to plan with that future in mind.

First, set aside high-reaching pet dreams, like wanting your child to attend Harvard or become an Olympic athlete or a Nobel Prize winner. Nothing is impossible, but allowing a child to follow their own dreams, as opposed to placing specific expectations for them at a young age, is a hallmark of good parenting. So, how can you best prepare your child to achieve their highest goals, their fullest potential?

By beginning with the end in mind.

There are certain key characteristics you will want to foster to help your children become productive workers, upstanding citizens, and most importantly, happy adults. Having these qualities will enable them to have the life they want.

Productive adults manage their time wisely and complete tasks necessary for work and home life. Your child can learn to follow a visual schedule and to finish school activities and household chores. Reinforce helpfulness and a solid work ethic in specific ways. For example, rather than saying, "You are so helpful!" try instead, "I like the way you helped your sister find her lost toy." Instead of a generic "Good work," tell your child, "I saw how you kept working on that puzzle even when it was hard!"

Upstanding citizens have learned to make wise choices and accept responsibility for their actions. Your child can learn to make good choices, too. Establish developmentally appropriate expectations for your child's behavior, and provide positive feedback and reinforcement when you see them moving toward those expectations. Redirect and teach better options when your child engages in unwanted behaviors.

A happy adult has developed a positive outlook. You can help your child be happier by letting them feel safe, loved, and valued. If your child struggles to cope with change, you can help by preparing them for expectations in new situations and by not springing surprises on them!

Your child feels loved when you remind them that your love for them is unconditional. Do not assume they know. Tell them that when they act out and behave in unacceptable ways, you will always love them, despite your disapproving of their behaviors.

Your child feels valued when you honor their passions and show interest in what they love. If you emphasize areas of weakness while ignoring strengths, they may come to doubt their own competence. When you acknowledge and build on strengths and listen to them tell you again about all the different kinds of dinosaurs, they will learn to value themselves as you value them.

To foster a calm, non-aggressive adult, do not tolerate any hitting now of you or anyone else. Model appropriate responses such as "Ow!" or "I'm mad!" or use nonverbal but non-touching expressions of larger feelings such as stamping a foot instead of kicking.

If you do not want an adult who spends excessive time indoors in front of a screen, then promote active outdoor play now. Put down your own phone and go for a walk, toss a ball in the yard, ride bikes, or have an impromptu family dance party.

If you do not want an adult who says "I can't" or "You do it for me," then do not perform the tasks they should be doing for themselves. Yes, it will take a lot longer to put on their own shoes and socks, especially while they are learning. But you do not want to tie the shoes of your future teenager or adult, do you? Teach them, show them, perform some of the steps and let them take over gradually, until you can step back and congratulate them for doing it all by themselves. Their feeling of pride and accomplishment will be worth it!

Wherever you are on your parenting journey, and whatever age your child is right now, look forward and plant seeds for the future, beginning with the end in mind.

Nelson Mandela said, "We are born to manifest the glory of God that is within us. It is not just in some of us—it is in everyone." Our shared goal is to honor the glory in all of us and enhance each child's journey to their fullest potential. If this book helps that process in any way, our purpose will be served. If you are now confused and overwhelmed, you need a compassionate and optimistic plan for the early years and beyond. Where to start?

Right here.

PART I
First Steps

They Say It's Autism …
What Does That Mean?

"Autism can't define me. I define autism."

— *Kerry Magro, author with autism*

Chapter 1

Hearing the News

"If you've met one person with autism,
you've met *one* person with autism."

— *Dr. Stephen Shore, author, speaker, and professor with autism*

Every parent remembers the moment they first met their baby, whether in a birthing center, delivery room, government office, or adoption agency. There is an instant bond of love and connection that overrides every other emotion.

Parents of children with autism also remember the intensity of emotion they experienced the first time someone told them their child's diagnosis. It can be overwhelming, and parents often experience shock and disbelief. Hundreds of questions leap instantly to mind as they try to imagine what lies ahead. Many have little to no experience with autism and what the diagnosis will mean for their child, for them, and for the family.

Parents need to learn what to expect and where to find help and support. Once they know where they are going, they can move forward, armed with knowledge, hope, and the assurance that they will not be alone on this venture. Dedicated mentors, autism professionals, teachers, and most importantly, the love and understanding of friends and family, are essential components of the treatment and coping process. This learning will continue throughout the child's early years, childhood, adolescence, and transition to adulthood as the family learns more about autism and how to succeed at every stage of the journey.

Upon hearing the news about autism for the first time, your first question is likely to be, "What is autism, anyway?" Autism Spectrum Disorder (ASD) is a group of neurobiological conditions resulting from a transaction between a biologically predisposed individual and an array of possible environmental influences. It is a condition that impacts a child's social communication capacity. There are multiple ways these challenges can manifest, to varying degrees of severity.

Your child has a rainbow of strengths as well as challenges. Stephen Shore famously said, "If you've met one person with autism you've met one person with autism." This is because children with ASD are unique, just like typically developing children. We cannot label a child and from that determine their abilities, nor can we make any guesses as to their outcomes. Be wary of those who purport to have a "crystal ball." One of our mentors used to say that if you want to find out how an 18-year-old will turn out, take a good look at them at 17 years old, and then guess!

But you probably have more questions. Here are some answers.

What causes ASD?

We do not have all the answers yet, but we do know this:

- *Autism is not your fault,* and it is not your partner's fault.

- *Autism is not contagious;* no one has ever "caught" autism.

- *Autism is not caused by parenting mistakes;* spoiling children does not create autism.

- *Autism is not caused by immunizations,* or by antibiotics or ultrasounds.

- *Predisposition:* Children with ASD are genetically predisposed to having the disorder.

- *Environmental impacts* are being studied but the answers are still not in.

- *Genes and environmental factors* constantly interact and are the subject of ongoing research.

When does ASD start?

About 2 out of 3 children with autism appear to show symptoms and signs of ASD from very early on, even from birth. Some parents report typical development until around two years of age, followed by a loss of skills, or what has been called 'regression.'

Other individuals with strengths in language and cognition might be able to mask areas of weakness, so that they remain undiagnosed until the middle school years or even later into adulthood. This does not mean they suddenly "developed autism," but rather that their ability to imitate typically developing peers was enough to get them by and to fly under the radar of autism screening, at least up until social communication pressures resulted in the symptoms becoming more apparent, such as group learning in school.

What is normal development?

AGE:	WHAT TO EXPECT:	WHEN TO BE CONCERNED:
1 year	plays pat-a-cake and peek-a-boo points to things they like or want uses sounds as words, like "mama" for mother or "baba" for bottle waves bye-bye to people	does not yet engage in social play does not yet point or wave to people prefers objects over people does not yet say "mama" or "bye-bye" avoids looking at your face when you talk or play with them
2 years	speaks at least 50 words uses two-word phrases is 50% understandable follows simple two-step directions imitates adult actions and words enjoys playing with toys shows interest in other children	does not respond to name or questions has few words and no phrases places your hand on an object to get help does not look at a person to get help does not imitate others does not play with toys typically ignores or does not notice other children

AGE:	WHAT TO EXPECT:	WHEN TO BE CONCERNED:
3 years	has 300 words, 75% understood uses three-word phrases uses words socially to connect knows their own first name dresses with little help feeds themselves enjoys playing near or with others enjoys trying to be independent	has few spoken words does not yet put words together does not use words to interact with others does not respond to "What's your name?" takes off clothes but does not try to dress self needs help with feeding avoids or ignores other children has problems with toilet training
4 years	speaks in phrases of 4 words uses 1000 words, 100% understood gives first and last name if asked tells about an event that happened enjoys interactive and pretend play	does not yet speak in sentences uses far fewer than 1000 words does not yet answer questions does not yet tell about what happened prefers solitary, repetitive play or activity

What if my child is behind on these milestones?

Remember that all children develop at their own pace. There is no need to be concerned if your child is not developing in lockstep with their siblings, cousins, or neighbors. Don't panic about a small lag in development; kids grow in spurts and tend to catch up on their own timetable.

If your child is not in school yet and you have concerns, discuss any areas you see as possibly delayed with your child's doctor. The doctor may take a medical history and conduct a physical examination to identify or rule out medical conditions that might cause developmental delays, which may account for the symptoms. Screening for ASD is also performed, and then a determination is made regarding whether a developmental assessment is warranted.

If your child is in school, teachers will be aware if there is a gap between where your child is and where other children their age are. If the delay is significant, they may refer your child for psycho-educational assessment.

What is involved in an autism assessment?

A developmental assessment to diagnose ASD usually has three components: observations, interviews, and formal or informal tests and measures.

It is important for children to be observed in their natural learning environments. School-aged children may be observed in the classroom and on the playground.

If your child is not yet in school, assessment teams may make home visits; however, this is not always possible. This is where you come in. No one knows your child better than you do, and you have seen them in all kinds of settings, at home and in the community. Your point of view is invaluable.

Interviews are an important way for the evaluator to get input from those who know your child best. Parents' and caregivers' inputs are vital. For school-aged children, the teacher's input will provide insight into how they respond in the classroom and playground s settings. Questionnaires may be used to gather school information.

In addition to observations and interviews, formal and informal tests and measures are usually a part of an ASD assessment. There is no single definitive test for ASD, but there are many tests that provide information about whether an individual has ASD. Your clinician will choose which of them to use for your particular situation.

What autism tests might be used?

Screening tests to identify children at risk for ASD are performed in doctors' offices. This process has been recommended by the American Academy of Pediatrics. Other tests are used in school or clinical settings. Here are some of the more common tests that might be used:

- *M-CHAT-R Modified Checklist for Autism in Toddlers, Revised* is a commonly used screening test for 18- to 24-month-old toddlers. It is not a diagnostic test, but it will let you know whether your child is at risk for ASD and whether a comprehensive assessment is warranted.

- *ADOS-2 Autism Diagnostic Observation Schedule, Second Edition (ADOS-2)* is considered a "gold standard" diagnostic measure.

It is a semi-structured, standardized test of communication, social interaction, play, and restricted and repetitive behaviors based on how the child responds and interacts with the assessor and the available toys and objects during the assessment. Remember, no test alone is sufficient to make a diagnosis.

- *ADI-R Autism Diagnostic Interview Revised* may be used as a companion to the ADOS-2. It is a standardized, semi-structured, comprehensive interview guide for parents or caregivers. Other tests which may be used include:

- *CARS-2 Childhood Autism Rating Scale, Second Edition*

- *ASRS Autism Spectrum Rating Scales*

- *SCQ Social Communication Questionnaire*

- *ASQ-3 Ages & Stages Questionnaires, Third Edition*

- *MIGDAS-2 Monteiro Interview Guidelines for Diagnosing Autism Spectrum, Second Edition (MIGDAS-2).*

In addition to these ASD tests, further testing of cognitive capacity and adaptive functioning is often part of the overall assessment. Once the assessment is completed, the *Diagnostic and Statistical Manual of Mental Disorders, Fifth Edition* (DSM-5) criteria are reviewed, and if these criteria are met, then the individual is diagnosed with ASD.

Do not be shy about asking questions when the evaluator goes over the assessment plan with you; you are an important part of this assessment, and you should know what to expect.

How do they know if my child has autism?

As stated above, the bottom line in determining whether your child has ASD is the diagnostic criteria in the (DSM-5). That sounds like a mouthful, and maybe a little intimidating, but it is simply a guide that doctors, clinical psychologists, and other evaluators use for diagnosing various conditions including ASD. The DSM-5 says that a person with ASD has "persistent deficits in social interaction and social communication," along with "restricted, repetitive patterns of behavior, interests, or activities." These symptoms must have been present in the early developmental years, even if they were not noticed until later in life, and they must cause "significant impairment in social, occupational, or other important areas of current functioning."

Test scores alone do not tell the story, but they give the clinical specialist the information needed to determine whether a child meets these criteria.

What other conditions might go along with autism?

ASD rarely travels alone. Many people with autism have other conditions which often, but not always, co-occur with ASD.

- *ADHD.* One of the most common concurrent disorders in children is attention-deficit/hyperactivity disorder (ADHD): both the inattentive and impulsive-hyperactive presentation. It's normal for young children to have trouble focusing their attention, to have a high activity level, and to follow their impulses without thinking things through. However, if these behaviors are extreme compared to other same-aged children's and compromise day-to-day functioning in two or more settings, it could become a problem.

- *Anxiety* is also very commonly seen in children with ASD. Anxiety can manifest in many ways, including self-injurious behaviors and temper outbursts.

- *OCD.* Obsessive-compulsive disorder (OCD) may cause a child to fixate on one idea or activity and have trouble switching gears.

- *ODD.* Oppositional defiant disorder (ODD) may look like saying "no" to everything.

- *Physical problems* such as constipation, diarrhea, tics, and even seizures can be seen. But, we'll discuss more on these later.

What other conditions mimic ASD?

Your clinician will attempt to rule out or identify other conditions which may be mistaken for ASD. If your child only has some, and not all, of the symptoms of autism, they might have another disorder, such as:

- *Social Communication Disorder*

- *Global Developmental Delay*

- *Language Delay*

- *Social Anxiety Disorder*

- *Nonverbal Learning Disability*

Although these conditions share many symptoms, these other disorders are not ASD. ASD is a collection of characteristics that are consistent with the DSM-5 diagnostic criteria, all of which must be met.

The bottom line: be aware and learn all you can, but do not waste today worrying about what might or might not happen in the future. Write down any questions, and make sure you ask them at your next visit with your primary care doctor or autism specialist.

Chapter 2

Responding to the News

"Your living is determined not so much by what
life brings to you as by the attitude you bring to
life; not so much by what happens to you as by
the way your mind looks at what happens."

— *Kahlil Gibran*

How do you respond?

You have just learned that your child has autism. There are probably
dozens of emotions running through you right now, many of which
are conflicting and overwhelming. If one of them is anger or denial,
even though your child is alive and otherwise healthy, does that make
you a terrible parent? No, of course not. All emotions are valid and
should be acknowledged. Grieving a sudden change in the parenting
journey you imagined does not in any way diminish your love for your
child. In fact, your unconditional love will help you survive the challenges any parent feels when their child is threatened. Your personal
map of road bumps just comes with a name: autism.

You may experience the same stages of grief that people go through
when mourning any loss, including the death of a parent, a sibling, or
even a child. These stages do not necessarily follow any order. There is
no right or wrong way, no formula that predicts what happens.

- **Denial.** How can your adorable, loving child have autism? Surely there must be a mistake. Maybe the doctor got it wrong, or your child was having an off day, or you exaggerated your concerns. You may cling to the memories of every time your child made eye contact or showed love for you or laughed at something silly. How can they have autism if they can do all these things and react in those ways? It is because autism is not just one thing; it is a collection of symptoms or characteristics. Your child might have many strengths and still meet the diagnostic criteria for autism. You might think of going ahead and getting a second or third opinion, and that is okay if it helps you process the reality. In time, you will be ready to move forward to help your child be the best they can be. Sadly, some are stuck in the denial phase.

- **Anger.** It is devastating to be told that there is "something wrong" with your beloved child, and that the problem might be lifelong indeed. During these times, it is not uncommon for that anger to be directed at the messenger, the one who suspected autism, or the one who made the diagnosis. It can be directed toward family members, oneself, or even your child. These feelings are normal and not at all unusual, but be careful not to act out those feelings by lashing out at your loved ones. They need you, and you need them. Working together as part of your child's team will optimize your child's outcome.

- **Bargaining.** If you pray hard enough or if you ensure your child gets 40 hours a week of therapy, will things, please, be different?

If you adhere to that specialized diet you read about online and buy all the vitamins you have heard of, will the autism please just go away? Remember: this is your child. Love them for who they are, warts and all. Wishing away their autism is like wishing for a different child, and every child deserves to be accepted and loved for exactly who they are!

- *Depression.* Parents might feel sad at the loss of the dream they had hoped for before the child was born. Despite any suffering you may feel, know that this is about not you, but your child. Depression is treatable; get the help you need, so you can be the parent you want to be.

- *Acceptance* is the final stage. As you learn more about autism and your child's unique needs, you will rise to the occasion and be their champion. You can take your rightful place as a parent who can and will make a difference in your child's life!

These stages of grief are experienced differently by every parent. Depending on the stage of grieving, misunderstandings can arise, which can cause marital conflict. Accept your partner and respect where they are coming from. There are no right or wrong answers in the grieving process.

How does your partner take the news?

Every couple has their share of stress, and when a child is diagnosed with ASD, there is no doubt that the relationship can be impacted. If one parent becomes the autism expert, the other may feel left out and neglected. Can your relationship survive this? Yes, it can. But you need to remember what is important, to choose your battles, and to learn how to let the little things go. Keep these tips in mind:

- *Focus on each other.* A balanced, mindful relationship can prevent "emotional divorce."

- *Respect boundaries.* Allow each other time alone when needed.

- *Support success.* Positively affirm each partner's role and contribution.

- *Nurture romance.* Go out on dates with your partner.

The more you share your feelings and needs with each other, the more support, insight, and understanding you get back in return. Look for a support group for parents or couples living with a child with autism. Seeking out and accepting help is the smart thing to do.

How does this affect your other children?

Any time there is a new baby in the family, siblings are affected. Things change, including their position in the family and the pecking order. When a child is diagnosed with ASD, it usually means that much of parents' time and energy is focused on that child, and consequently, siblings may feel left out. Additionally, they may feel resentful, angry, frightened, or embarrassed by their sibling's behaviors. They may believe that they should not complain, since they were fortunate enough to be born without a disability. Guilt is very common. Recognize and acknowledge all these feelings. Let your child's siblings know that resentment and embarrassment are common, along with typical responses experienced by many siblings with a special needs brother or sister.

As they get older, especially if their sibling with ASD needs a significant amount of daily support, they may worry, often realistically, that they will need to become the full-time caregiver or responsible partner after their parents are gone. Whether they embrace or dread this possibility, they should be reassured that there are many support options.

Be aware that siblings of children with ASD have a much greater chance of having autism than do children in the general population. Additionally, they are at risk for other neurodevelopmental difficulties, such as social anxiety and learning disabilities. When one child is diagnosed, siblings with fewer or less noticeable symptoms may not be referred for assessment. They may seem fine when compared to a sibling with ASD, but nonetheless may still have significant social communication challenges and even be falling behind their typical peers.

Look for a sibling-support program for your typically developing children. If your child's school does not have one, maybe you can help start one.

What do you tell the grandparents?

Grandparents are among your child's greatest cheerleaders, and they may also be in the greatest denial. Their perfect grandchild could not possibly have autism, and they may even accuse you of trying to "make" them disabled. A "self-fulfilling prophecy," they might say. Be patient with them as they learn more about autism and how it affects their precious darling. Once they understand, grandparents often become your staunchest allies.

Consider writing a letter disclosing the diagnosis and what it may mean for your child. Share this letter with extended family and close friends. They probably want to know how they can help, and by sharing, they might learn a thing or two. Knowledge is a powerful coping tool.

How can you get the support you need?

- **Ask.** Do not say no to any offers of help. It doesn't make you a "bad parent" if you allow concerned friends and family members to help with the laundry, bring in a meal, or offer to babysit so you can get some much-needed rest and relaxation. Plus, they feel better when they can be useful.

- **Practice** stress-management and coping strategies such as exercise, meditation, or yoga.

- **Nurture** your spiritual side. Remind yourself of the things you are thankful for every day and maintain an attitude of gratitude.

- **Stay connected** by nurturing friendships outside the family.

- **Stay healthy** by getting enough sleep, exercise, and nutrition, and by staying hydrated.

- **Reach out.** Find a counselor, support group, or parent mentor who has made this journey before you.

Remember that the child you have loved since the day they were born is the same child after you hear the news about autism. Nothing important has changed. Doors will now open for your child—doors to understanding, services, and support. Remember, you have power over how you respond to the news. Focus on the positives and redirect negative or pessimistic thinking. You have much to be thankful for.

Chapter 3

Looking Forward (Oh, for a crystal ball.)

*"The best way to predict your future
is to create it."*

— Abraham Lincoln

Will my child ever...?

At the time of diagnosis, a myriad of questions arises. Will my child ever speak? Will they go to school with the other kids in their neighborhood? Will they graduate, go to college, get a job, get married, give us grandchildren? There is so much information on the internet. A lot of it sounds scary on the one hand, but on the other hand, it is not necessarily true.

Some individuals with ASD have indeed achieved each of these goals, and while they do not all do so, typically developing children might not achieve all these milestones, either. We do not know what any child will be capable of in the future. We do not have a crystal ball.

So, what about your child? We have learned that the brain is plastic and that skills can come online at different ages and stages. Windows of opportunity remain open for many years, and certainly early intervention is the best course of action. No matter how old your child is when they are first diagnosed, it is never too late to begin the intervention process. Gains can be made no matter when they start. Therefore, we must advocate for support services throughout the life span.

There is no intervention and coping tool more powerful and effective than education. Learn all you can about autism and how it affects your child. Study how your child learns best and what they love to do. Notice any obstacles to their progress and work on removing them. We are often blown away by parents who, on day one of the diagnosis, are totally overwhelmed with feelings of loss and inadequacy, but very soon after that, become amazing advocates on behalf of their children. You are the sun in your child's firmament. The professionals play their roles, but you are your child's first and best teacher. Step up, get involved, take charge!

Start with the end in mind.

What do we really want for our children? That they be happy, fulfilled and reach their optimal potential. This is no different for a child with ASD. The end goal we are looking toward is an independent adult. Initially, at the time of diagnosis, they may need a lot of help, but that will not last forever. For every task you do for them now, think of how you can teach them to do more and more of it themselves, even though it is often easier and quicker for you to do it for them. Feed your child now the way you would like to see them eating as teenagers. For every misbehavior that you allow to become ingrained, imagine them doing the same thing as an 18-year-old. Would that be acceptable? Could they even be arrested for it? How would that behavior interfere with relationships or employment? If it would be a problem in adulthood, you need to address the behaviors early on. Right now! Anytime you want to put an end to a behavior, replace it with a skill which would obviate the need to exhibit the behavior in the first place. Does she constantly blow raspberries because she is fascinated by how the saliva droplets sparkle in the sunshine? Hand her a sparkly snow globe or other toy that provides the same visual effect to distract and redirect her from spitting.

Here are some tips for teaching "right" from the start:

- **Keep perspective.** You are dealing with a child, first and foremost. Are they just acting their age?

- **Analyze intent.** Every behavior has a communicative intent. What is your child trying to communicate?

- **Accentuate the positive.** Provide reinforcement for desired behaviors.

- **Build self-esteem** by seeking out strengths. What preferred behaviors do they exhibit? What are they good at? Provide opportunities for them to explore their own passions.

- **Provide consequences** for unwanted behaviors. Do not use ASD as an excuse for poor behavior choices. If a behavior is dangerous for your child, others, or property, you must address the behavior.

- **Understand** the difference between poor behavior choices and lack of readiness or ability. If a child is unable to do what you request, consider breaking the task down into smaller baby steps, and teach and reinforce each step one at a time. Be patient; learning new skills takes time. If a child does not yet have the prerequisite skills, you may need to pull back and begin with a task that will have a chance of succeeding. Avoid frustrating your child, or yourself for that matter. For instance, if your child does not appear to notice whether they have soiled themselves, and they do not have prerequisite skills needed for toilet training such as pulling down pants, they're probably not ready for toilet training—yet. Do not worry; just because they do not have readiness for that skill right now does not mean they never will. The day will come soon when they will succeed. The bottom line is, if they can do it, expect it. If they cannot do it yet, teach it once they exhibit the appropriate readiness skills.

- ***Structure the environment.*** Provide fun and constructive ways for your child to do what they love. Do they gleefully rip up pages of books and any other paper they get their hands on? Give them old mail to be shredded and let them tear it up for you. Do they love to jump on the bed? A small trampoline is a wonderful alternative, but if you do not have one, designate a safe "jumping spot" in your home where they can jump in place for as long as they need to.

- ***Anticipate*** problem behaviors before they arise and plan to head them off before they manifest. Does your child become upset and disruptive when they are made to sit at the table and maybe wait even a moment for their meal to be served? Plan to have their plate already at their seat, with at least one item you know they love to eat, before you call them to sit down. Does your child melt down when running errands with you? Provide a pictorial list of where you must go that day, ending with something you know they would enjoy.

- **Focus.** Get your child's attention before giving directions. Yes, you may need to cross the room and get right down at eye level, say their name, and perhaps touch their arm so they turn their attention away from their activity and engage with you. Once you have their attention, provide short, simple directions. Speak slowly. If they have the skills, ask them to repeat the instructions back, then send them off to do it. That way they might be able to process your request more efficiently. When they are fully engaged in a favorite activity, no amount of cajoling or yelling at them from across the room will get them to stop and look at you. Do not frustrate yourself and them by expecting the impossible. This does not mean you will never be able to talk to them from across the room and get a response, just that you need to start where they are now, then build from there. Baby steps.

- **Relax.** Teach relaxation skills when they are relaxed, not in the middle of a meltdown. If they have practiced mindful breathing or counting or singing a calming song many times, then when you ask them to do it during a stressful time, they will be able to remember and use the strategy. More on this later.

- **Use positive language.** Do not tell them what not to do; tell them what to do instead. For example, instead of "Don't run," say "Walk." Rather than shouting "Stop yelling," try whispering "Use a mouse voice." Name the behavior you want to see, not the misbehavior, so they will know what is expected.

Hope.

Never give up hope on your child. We cannot guess which child will improve and to what extent, and we continue to be pleasantly surprised. Now, it might not be the exact future you envisioned when your child was born, but this is about them, not you. We need to celebrate each child for who they are and cheer on every step to success they exhibit, no matter how teeny. It was always going to be their journey, not yours. Your child will learn and grow in their own way and in their own time. Having autism means their brain is different, and they may learn in their own unique ways. Rather than trying to reshape your child into your idea of "normal," appreciate the many things that make them so wonderfully lovable. Honor, respect, and celebrate who they are, give them the tools they need, and you can help them achieve the goals they will create for themselves. We do not have a crystal ball, but you may be pleasantly surprised by what the future holds in store for your amazing child.

PART II
Home Base

*Create an Environment
that Works for Everyone*

"Let your home be your mast and not your anchor."
— *Kahlil Gibran*

Chapter 4

Home, Safe Home

"Home is where we should feel secure and comfortable."

— Catherine Pulsifer, author

We spend much of our time at home eating, sleeping, and playing. It is our command center, our base, comfort zone, and cozy retreat all rolled up into one! But now, with an active toddler who knows no rules or bounds, we need to take extra precautions that would otherwise not be needed. Your home, sweet home needs to become your home, safe home!

Extreme childproofing for the Houdini household.

A safe home is not just a haven from the stresses of the world. We are talking about actual, physical safety. If you have older children, you already know the ropes of baby-proofing the house, but is your home prepared for a child whose uncanny visualization skill gives them superpowers to circumvent even your best safety efforts?

Let us begin with the basics:

- Install outlet plug covers, and check for overloaded outlets and frayed wires or cords.

- Put locks on cupboards that contain medicines, chemicals, or household cleaners.

- Keep knives and other dangerous tools out of reach.

- Tie up window pull-cords on blinds or curtains to avoid strangulation hazards.

- Secure bookshelves and tall furniture to the wall; many kids with ASD love to climb as high as they can.

- Keep water temperature at 120 degrees Fahrenheit so those who love to play in water will not accidentally burn themselves.

- Toss potentially poisonous house plants.

- Check smoke detectors' batteries and keep reminders to re-check.

- Use a fireplace screen if you have a fireplace. Never leave your child unattended in a room with a fire.

- Skid-proof the bathtub with decals or stick-on bathmats.

- Remove doors from old refrigerators or trunks.

- Know how to shut off the electricity in case of an emergency.

- Keep flashlights or lamps with batteries in case of a blackout. Do not use candles or kerosene lanterns for emergency lighting.

You may marvel at your child's Houdini-like skills at getting around every cupboard lock and outlet protector you set up. If your child is one of those brilliant visual thinkers who can picture how so-called "childproof" locks work, you will need to be vigilant and creative. When first installing safety locks in your home, do not leave your child alone in that room until you know the locks will be effective.

Elopement: it does not mean what you think it does.

The behavioral definition of "elopement" is to leave a designated area without permission, such as running out of a classroom or from a home. It is a sinking feeling to emerge from the bathroom only to find that in two minutes, your child has pushed boxes and furniture to the front door, climbed and unlatched the safety lock, and traveled halfway around the block. Children are resourceful and determined in their desire to seek out new places. Here are some tips to keep one step ahead of them:

- Install multiple deadbolts and chains high on each exterior door.

- Put locks on windows.

- Put bells or noisemakers on your child's door to awaken you if they wander during the night.

- Install locking fences around your yard and always around pools.

- Install alarms that go off each time an exterior door is opened.

Contain your car seat escape artist.

It seems some little people see a car seat as a personal challenge. How quickly can they unbuckle it and climb out? It is our job to keep them secured without endangering anyone.

Here are some car seat safety tips:

- Use the right size car seat for your child, installed correctly according to the manufacturer.

- Fasten all harness points securely, with the chest clip snugly at armpit level, not down around the tummy or up under the chin.

- While fastening your child, try to make it fun, such as pretending the car is a rocket ship. Create your own ritual around the buckling-in process that may include directions like "Arms up high! Touch the sky! Clap, clap, clap! Buckle goes snap!"

- Once your child is secured in the seat, immediately distract them from focusing on the buckle. Sing a favorite song, hand them a book, toy, or snack, ask them to find something out the window, or play favorite music.

- Reserve some highly desirable toys or snacks or videos for use in the car only. They will seem more special if they are never seen in the house.

- If they manage to unbuckle their car seat, immediately pull over. Maintain a calm and upbeat attitude while you re-buckle them, and if possible, return home, saying, "I see you don't want to be in the car seat right now, so we'll go home where I can take you out." Of course, it is not always feasible, but it helps if you can plan practice runs where you set off for the park but return home if the child unbuckles to try again the next day. Lesson learned!

Teach the safety skills they will need.

- Once they can, help your child memorize their address, parents' names, and phone numbers.

- Teach them the meaning of an emergency, how to dial 911 for a serious emergency, and whom they can ask for help when a situation does not require emergency services. For instance, if an adult falls and does not wake up, call 911. If you skin your knee, or if you cannot find something you need, ask a parent, not 911.

- Discuss "stranger danger" and what to do if approached by a stranger.

- Have fire drills and practice your EDITH (exit drill in the house.) Teach two ways to get out of any room.

- Teach that if they find a dangerous item such as matches, a lighter, or a weapon, they should tell an adult where it is and not let any child go near it.

- Teach kitchen safety, such as staying away from the stove and not playing near a parent while they are cooking.

- Practice what you teach. Model wearing a helmet when riding a bike, scooter, or skateboard.

With attention to these safety needs and details, your home can become a place of safety as well as a place of shelter and security.

Chapter 5

Home, Sweet School

"In an ideal world, schools might model themselves
after the home environment— the primary and natural
setting in which children learn and thrive."

— Connor Boyack, author

Home is the child's first classroom, and parents are their first teachers. Your cozy world begins to expand when your child is diagnosed. Soon, you may find a parade of behavior therapists, speech and occupational therapists, teachers, and others whose treatment services have been recommended for your child.

Will your child have any or all of these services? Will your program look exactly like that of a friend's child or what you have read about? It is not a one-size-fits-all approach. Your child's services may be as personal and unique as your child. A multi-modal approach incorporating various interventions is helpful.

Everyone involved in your child's care is on the same team. Clear communication across therapies is vital. Do not forget: your child is the most important person on the team, and you are your child's best advocate. Including the child and their perspective in the treatment process is vital every step of the way. Even if nonverbal, remember that all behaviors have communicative intent. Learn to read these nonverbal messages, however subtle. Think deeply about the meaning and intent of their actions. Assess their comfort level with the various therapies. Help therapists adopt that same approach. By adapting and individualizing intervention methods, we can all best meet the child's unique learning style and needs.

What kinds of programs are there?

- *Home-based programs* may be appropriate for younger children, allowing the child to remain in a comfort zone while a parent can observe and learn from experienced therapists.

- *Center-based* therapy may be combined with home programs or used instead of them. This may include opportunities for your child to interact with other children. Having typical peers who serve as language, social, and behavioral models is important. If your center does not offer this, seek out opportunities for your child to be around other children their age.

- *School-based programs* may be offered by your district, depending on your child's age and the availability of services. A school setting allows children to learn school routines, such as story time on the rug, and how to play with others at recess. Again, every attempt should be made to integrate the child into the typical mainstream environment. This should start from the very outset.

What are the different kinds of therapies?

- *Applied Behavior Analysis (ABA)* is the practical application of the science of behavior analysis. ABA therapies are usually supervised by Board-Certified Behavior Analysts (BCBA) and may be provided in homes, in centers, and in the school setting. Many evidence-based therapies are based on ABA principles.

- *Naturalistic Developmental Behavioral Interventions (NDBI)* are implemented in natural settings such as the home or neighborhood. NDBI uses a variety of ABA strategies to teach developmentally appropriate and prerequisite skills in natural environments. Rather than being adult-driven, NDBI involves shared control between child and therapist. It utilizes natural contingencies; for example, a therapist may work on blowing to strengthen muscles used in speech production. When the child successfully blows on a bubble wand, the reinforcement is the creation of bubbles. This is a more natural contingency than if the adult gives the child a treat or token for blowing.

- *Intensive Behavioral Intervention (IBI)* implements ABA services intensively and are provided for 20 hours a week or more.

- *Discrete Trial Training (DTT)* uses ABA to teach new skills in simplified, structured steps.

- *Pivotal Response Treatment (PRT)* is a naturalistic intervention that uses developmental approaches along with the principles of ABA to develop pivotal behaviors that need to be taught. These open the doors to teaching new behaviors, such as asking for help or emotional regulation.

- *Treatment and Education of Autistic and related Communication-Handicapped CHildren (TEACCH)* from the University of North Carolina utilizes visual learning and structured educational materials to enhance the quality of life for individuals with ASD and their families across the lifespan. Techniques such as visual schedules can be incorporated in early childhood programs, although many adults with ASD benefit from these approaches as well.

- **Social Stories™**, also called social scripts or social narratives, were developed by Carol Gray to help children with ASD understand social rules and to provide a guide for self-management in specific social situations. They can easily be modified to help children "pre-learn" responses to almost any challenging social or behavioral situation.

What are home-based services like?

Having professionals coming in and out of your home like a revolving door can feel extremely disruptive. If it is 10:00, the doorbell must be the behavioral therapist. If this is Tuesday, it must be the OT! Keeping track of the many players and their appointment schedules can feel chaotic. It is daunting to manage it all and maintain the kind of structured home setting that you enjoy and that your child appreciates. Daunting, but possible!

How can I create structure out of chaos?

- **Organize.** Keep a binder for your child's services, with dividers for assessments, medical records, educational paperwork like an Individualized Education Program (IEP), and a section for each of the agencies and therapists who work with your child.

- **Visualize.** Write down all appointments in a master calendar, such as a white board or a large wall calendar. This can be placed where the whole family can see it.

- **Picture it.** Make an easy-to-read calendar or visual schedule for your child, and show it to them daily. It is calming and reassuring for a child to know ahead of time what to expect. Take pictures of the therapists and add them to the days they will arrive. This prepares a child before the doorbell rings. Just point to the person's picture on the calendar. That is pre-learning!

- **A special place.** If possible, create a small, special workplace for your child, just for working with their therapists. Ask therapists about the need for floor space or table space, or any specific materials.

- **A special treat.** Have small bags of a child's favorite snacks available for reinforcements while working with your child. Use snacks that are not eaten every day—something a bit special.

- **Be assertive!** Talk to the therapists about your child's unique needs and whether they had a poor night's sleep or are having a good day. Help them understand if your child needs extra time to warm up before jumping right in.

- **Share** observations about your child's sensory needs. Do they crave certain sensory experiences, such as flashing lights, music boxes, scented objects to sniff, bubbles, or super soft toys? Therapists may want to use these as rewards to reinforce positive behaviors or skills. On the other hand, does your child cover their eyes at bright lights, cover their ears at unexpected sounds, avoid touching things like finger paints, or gag at odors? Avoid using potentially aversive stimuli during sessions.

- ***Success!*** Set your child up for successful learning experiences. You know your child best, and your insights are valuable.

What about sensory experiences?

Many children with ASD have unique responses to sensory stimuli. They may seek out some sensory experiences and strongly avoid others. In your home classroom, you can create structured experiences to meet your child's sensory needs.

Pay attention to the kinds of sensory experiences your child craves that they can do for hours at a time. Set up activities that use these as reinforcements when completing a challenging task or to help them calm down when they start to become overwhelmed. For example, if a child just loves watching the credits rolling at the end of a TV show even more than the show itself, and they want to rewind it again and again, they are likely seeking repetitive visual stimulation. Here is a PowerPoint trick you can try.

- Create a mini PowerPoint slideshow to scroll words you type, such as the child's name, any vocabulary words related to a lesson, or words of encouragement such as "Awesome!" or "You did it!"

- Re-type the word or phrase once per line until you have filled the slide.

- Now go to Animations, More Entrance Effects, and select Credits.

- Watch how quickly it scrolls on the Animation Pane.

- Try different speeds to see what your child likes best.

Now, when they have completed a task during a learning session, a reward can be watching the words scroll up the screen—a sensory activity you know they love, modified by you to make it meaningful and related to the skills you are trying to teach. You did it!

It is a good idea to remove or reduce the types of sensory input that bother your child. For example, if they tend to melt down every time the doorbell rings, cover your doorbell with a sign that says, "Do not ring bell, please knock," at least during in-home sessions. If bothered by the smell of food cooking, avoid cooking during session times. Make your child's session time a no-TV time for everyone—parents and siblings included. It is hard to focus when the theme song of a favorite show is playing down the hall. Many of our kids have superb hearing, and a closed door and lowered volume may not be enough.

How do I prepare for this revolving door of therapists coming to my home?

Having strangers come to your home and work with your child is a new experience, and certainly a mixed blessing.

On one hand, your child is finally getting the help they need and deserve. That is a wonderful feeling if you have been trying for a long time to get access to services. Your hard work paid off, and you are getting the help you need.

On the other hand, it is a challenge to gracefully share your home with people that you did not even interview for the job. You are being asked to trust others to provide you with reputable therapists, and you can only hope you will get along with them. If you and your child grow to not only accept but really like and enjoy them, you must also be prepared for them to move on and have another worker take their place. This is not easy, but it is worth seeing your child make gains and learn new skills, at whatever pace is right for them.

At the end of the day, this is your home and your child's safe haven. You have the right to ask questions, know what goals are being worked on, and give your input on goals that are important to you. You have the right to request a different therapist if you cannot agree with one. You have every right to decide who should and should not be working with your child.

Welcome the new vision of your home as your child's first classroom, while you take your rightful place as their first teacher, best advocate, and strongest supporter.

Chapter 6

Home, Sweet Home

"Home, sweet home. This is the place to find happiness."
— *M. K. Soni, author*

We all live here.

Your home is your castle and your family's sanctuary, safety zone, and home base. Perhaps this holds truest for your child with ASD. It may be a classroom or therapy space by day, but when all is said and done, your home belongs to you and your family. When parents return from work, or work from home for that matter, and when siblings return from school, home is the place where everyone can wind down, take off the masks and make-up, and just be themselves. Together. A sweet reality.

The flip side of letting down one's guard when safely ensconced at home is the relaxing of controls. After a full day of intense programming, your child is probably exhausted. The release of tension that results when demands are withdrawn may culminate in behavioral challenges. Recognize the clues signaling potential overload and be patient. Allow them a quiet place to unwind before new demands are placed on them. And remember the "Rule of Nines." Give praise nine times for every one correction! Now that is a challenge!

It is everyone's home, so each family member can help make it a loving, pleasant place. Do not let one child's needs disrupt the entire household. Let everyone pitch in on chores, but also include them in making fun decisions like dinner and dessert plans.

Let go of the perfect dream house to embrace the lived-in home.

Some of us have a utopian image of the home we envision for ourselves and our children. It usually looks organized, neat, and tidy, with a place for everything and everything in its place. This looks great in a magazine spread, but then reality strikes. Our family homes rarely resemble that glamorous vision. Let go of the perfect dream house and embrace the lived-in look that works for your family. Zero guilt!

One family we know set up elaborate, canvas-covered toy storage baskets neatly arranged on shelves. Art supplies were to go in one basket, building blocks in another, puzzles and plastic dishes and animals, each belonging in their own basket.

The problem was that room was constantly ankle-deep with every toy scattered on the floor. Their daughter strongly resisted putting the toys away or even touching the baskets.

Fortunately, those parents learned two things through observing their child and paying attention to her likes and dislikes. First, they had a very visual child who loved to see all her toys to know where they were. Second, their child had definite texture, tactile, and auditory aversions, and touching the canvas-covered baskets was actually painful to them, both in the feel of the rough canvas and in the sound it made when she brushed her hand across it, a sound which was not perceived by the parents but was painful to the child. That took a while to recognize!

The solution was to replace the canvas-lined baskets with clear plastic bins, and to clearly label each bin with a photo of the toys that belonged inside. Now the child could easily see all their toys without spreading them all on the floor, and there were no sensory barriers to putting toys away in the bins. Problem solved!

Thomas Jefferson said, "The happiest moments of my life have been the few which I have passed at home." At the end of the day, your home is your family's castle. Whatever level of clutter or organization works best for your family is yours to determine. Make your home truly a home, sweet home.

PART III
Healthy Habits
Start at Home

The Right Path from Day One

"Remember, the goal is not to raise great kids;
it's to raise kids who become great adults."

— *Andy Andrews, author, and speaker*

Chapter 7

Nutrition Needs

"Eating is living, and picky eaters should definitely
be nudged toward trying different foods little by little.
That's what I reckon, anyway."

— *Naoki Higashida, thirteen-year-old with autism, author of* The Reason I Jump

Beginning with the end in mind is our mantra, and nowhere is it more important than when feeding your child. As Naoki Higashida said, "Eating is living." It is quite an enigma why so many people with ASD have self-limited diets, along with unusual food preferences and aversions. This might be related to sensory sensitivities, not just pertaining to taste, but also to how food smells or looks, its textures, and even its colors and shapes. Parents must navigate the middle ground of gently encouraging and reinforcing children to try wider varieties of foods while avoiding power struggles and undue pressure that only serves to frustrate everyone.

What is good nutrition for my child?

- *Protein.* Offer your child a range of protein options to find their favorites. Consider seafood, lean meat and poultry, eggs, beans, peas, soy products, and unsalted nuts and seeds. Even if they do not like the texture of meat or chicken, they might enjoy fish sticks or chicken nuggets. Baking rather than frying is optimal.

- *Fruits.* Most children love naturally sweet fruit. Eating fresh, frozen, canned, or dried fruits is a better option than drinking fruit juice. If you do offer juice, dilute with water, limit servings, and ensure there is no added sugar or corn syrup. The same is true for canned fruits: check for added sugars! If your child enjoys dried fruit, remember that 1/4 cup of dried fruit counts as one cup of fruit, so watch the added calories. Moderation is best.

- *Vegetables.* Offer your child a wide array of fresh, canned, frozen, or even dried vegetables with colors ranging from dark green to red and orange. Ensure that canned or frozen vegetables are low in sodium. When you offer a tray of bite-sized, colorful vegetables presented in a fun, attractive way, you may find your child eating more of them.

- *Grains.* Whole grains, such as whole wheat bread, oatmeal, quinoa, brown or wild rice, and popcorn are great. Yes, popcorn is a whole grain! However, to avoid choking hazards, popcorn should be reserved for children over four or five years old. Limit refined grains such as white bread, rice, and pasta.

- *Dairy.* Low-fat or fat-free dairy products, including milk, yogurt, and cheeses, are a good choice. Watch for high sugar content in fruit yogurts; rather, offer plain yogurt with fresh fruit stirred in.

- *Limit added sugar,* including brown sugar, corn syrup, and honey. Use naturally occurring sugars in fruit and milk products in moderation. Some foods labeled "healthy," such as cereals, yogurts, and applesauce, contain added sugar. Read ingredient labels!

- **Limit saturated and trans fats.** Saturated fats mostly come from animals such as red meat, poultry, and full-fat dairy products. Try substituting saturated fats with vegetable and nut oils. Use healthy fats, such as avocados, nuts, and olives. Avoid partially hydrogenated oil.

How do I alleviate mealtime stress?

- **Routine.** Create a mealtime routine and stick to it. Eating at the same time and in the same place every day provides a sense of comfort and familiarity.

- **Comfort.** Make sure your child's seat, highchair, or booster is comfortable and at the right height for the table.

- **Familiarity.** While providing a range of healthy foods, always include at least one preferred familiar food.

- **Peace.** Avoid making dinner time a battleground. Do not insist that your child eat everything on the plate. For those with intense sensory aversions, no amount of coercion will persuade them to eat it, but it can make them resent coming to the table.

- **Independence.** Once your child can self-feed and drink from a cup, do not spoon-feed or hold the cup to their lips. It might be easier and neater to do it for them, but would you spoon-feed a kindergartner? A third grader? A teenager? Remember the adult you want your child to be. Feeding your child as you would an adult is the game plan. Provide utensils and a napkin. Once children have the manual dexterity to manipulate a spoon or fork, discourage finger-feeding.

- *Focus on family.* Create a positive, happy family atmosphere during dinner. Turn off all screens and avoid controversial or stressful topics of conversation. Bring interesting articles or pictures to share. Have special events, like Funny Hat Night or Tell a Joke Night. Let each person share the best thing that happened to them that day or talk about their favorite topic for a time while everyone listens.

What about picky eaters?

- *Relax.* Introduce new foods matter-of-factly by simply putting a small bite on the edge of the plate. At first, the goal is just for the child to get used to seeing the new food and seeing other family members eating it.

- *Baby steps.* Eventually proceed to having your child touch the new food, then another day smell it, then another day kiss it, later licking it, until they can take a tiny bite of it. Trying new foods by taking baby steps makes it easier to eventually accept and even enjoy the new food.

- *Ask* your behavioral therapist for reinforcement ideas for each of these baby steps.

If your child goes through all these steps and still does not enjoy the food, honor those personal preferences. We do not all like the same things. No adult would be happy being forced to eat foods they dislike.

What about food allergies and special diets?

- *Ask the doctor.* If you believe your child may be allergic to foods, consult with your primary care provider (PCP) or developmental pediatrician and follow their advice.

- *GFCF.* If recommended, diets such as the gluten-free and casein-free (GFCF) diet may help. A trial of a GFCF diet need last only six to eight weeks. Children on special diets should be monitored to address possible nutritional deficiencies, including those of calcium and Vitamins B and D, protein limitation, and lack of fiber, which can result in constipation.

- *Monitor.* Set appropriate expectations and accurately delineate specific treatment goals with your autism specialist to determine whether any special treatment is working.

- *Do not place* your child on a highly restrictive diet without consulting a doctor.

- *Buyer beware!* There is no diet which can "cure" autism, and if someone tries to persuade you of a cure, beware.

Should I worry about my child's constipation and diarrhea?

- *It is not unusual.* Chronic diarrhea and chronic constipation are commonly seen in ASD. Toe-walking might be an attempt to withhold stool. Stool soiling and abdominal discomfort can lead to irritability, and toilet training can be impacted. Once treated, a decrease in behavior problems might become apparent. Discuss this with your PCP.

- **Constipation.** Treatment of chronic constipation is primarily dietary. This is in your control, so watch your child's diet. Limit constipating foods such as dairy, highly processed foods, and sugary treats. Diets too light in fiber, such as white bread, are also culprits.

- **Increase** water intake, juices, vegetables, and fruits to alleviate constipation. Stool softeners may be needed; check with your doctor.

- **Diarrhea** is a common problem in young children. Severe diarrhea can lead to malnutrition and requires medical attention. Speak with your PCP.

- **Increase** bananas, rice, applesauce, and toast if your child has diarrhea.

- **Decrease** dairy products and fatty, spicy, fried, and highly processed foods.

What about other gastrointestinal conditions or complications?

- **Pica** is the swallowing of nonfood items, often found on the carpet or playground. Children with iron deficiency anemia or lead toxicity are particularly prone to pica. This condition might lead to parasitic infestations or other problems.

- **If severe** gastrointestinal (GI) or eating problems persist, including gagging and vomiting, a referral to a gastroenterologist is advisable.

The most important thing you can do for your child's nutritional health, besides feeding them balanced meals, is to maintain a positive attitude towards food. The way you meet their nutrition needs now lays the groundwork for the adult they will become. Enjoy healthy meals as a family gathered around the dinner table, sharing good conversation and positive feelings, and you will pave the way for healthy adult attitudes toward diet and nutrition.

Chapter 8

Exercise Needs

"Exercise daily. Exercise may come in fun forms such as jumping on a trampoline or just dancing ..."

— *Dr. Raun Melmed,* Autism and the Extended Family

Exercise is an important need for people of all ages. If you want your adult child to have an active, healthy life that includes physical exercise, the time to start is now. Make physical exercise part of your child's daily routine and part of your own, too. By modeling an active lifestyle, you show them how important it is to get moving. So, exercise daily!

Why do we need to exercise daily?

- *Mental health.* Exercise combats anxiety and depression. It improves quality of life—for both you and your child.

- *Physical health.* Exercise reduces risk for diabetes and heart disease. It has immediate and long-term health benefits.

- *Emotional well-being.* Exercise decreases stress and promotes a positive lifestyle.

How can I get my child involved?

- *Animals.* Name exercises after their favorite animals, like Caterpillar Crawl, Dinosaur Stomp, Kangaroo Jump, or Crab Walk.

- *Superheroes.* Does your child love a superhero? Modify jumping jacks to include superhero poses, arms on hips or stretched ahead as if flying, between each jump.

- *Interests.* Whatever your child's favorite subject is, incorporate it into an exercise. Get them involved to create and name the new exercises. If they created it, they are more likely to engage in the exercise.

- *Make exercise fun!*

How can I use my child's strong sensory preferences to make exercise fun?

- *Proprioceptive.* For children with strong proprioceptive needs, jumping on a trampoline will be fun. For those without a trampoline, jumping in place while holding hands with a parent is a great alternative. Doing push-ups against a wall is another way to provide proprioceptive feedback.

- *Visual.* If your child has visual interests and loves watching things move rhythmically, try dancing while holding a long ribbon that streams behind them, or a ribbon on a stick which they can use to "draw" in the air. This is a favorite of many!

- *Auditory.* Children with auditory strengths love music. Put on a favorite tune and dance the day away!

Why make exercise a family affair?

- *Unity.* The family that moves together grooves together!

- *Quality.* Exercising with your children is quality time well spent.

- *Laughter* can be great exercise for the heart, lungs, and abdominal muscles. Being silly while exercising together is doubly beneficial!

- *Fun!* An all-family random dance party gives everyone the chance to get moving!

When you exercise with your children, you teach them a valuable lesson. When they see you exercising, laughing, and having fun, children learn that this is a lifelong activity. You are creating a healthy, active future adult!

Chapter 9

Sleep Needs

"Sleep is the best meditation."

— *Dalai Lama*

Sixty to eighty percent of children with ASD have sleep-related challenges. Sleep deprivation directly impacts the child, but as any parent will tell you, it also affects everyone in the family. Children with ASD and other developmental challenges tend to learn new tasks more slowly, at least initially. That is why it is so important to set your child up for success very early on. Sleep hygiene routines need to be in place from infancy and be consistently applied.

You can create the lifelong habits that will be invaluable for your child at any age. Will structuring and consistently applying good sleep hygiene every night be inconvenient? Yes, there is no getting around that. This is not a quick or easy process at first; however, there are many delightful aspects to the process that you all might enjoy. Establishing the groundwork early will pay off later. If you want a teenager who can fall asleep independently and will not come to your bed if they awaken in the night, then now is the time to put in the effort to help establish good sleep patterns.

How much sleep should my child get?

CHILD'S AGE	AVERAGE HOURS OF SLEEP PER DAY
4–12 months	12–16 hours (including 2–3 naps)
1–2 years	11–14 (including 1–2 naps)
3–5 years	10–13 (including 0–1 nap)
6–12 years	9–12 hours
13–18 years	8–10 hours

What kinds of sleep problems are common for children with ASD?

- Difficulty winding down.

- Crying at bedtime.

- Difficulty initiating sleep.

- Unable to fall asleep alone in their room.

- Waking several times during the night, seeking company.

- Awakening extremely early in the morning and demanding attention.

- During the school years, difficulty waking up early enough for school.

What is a sleep hygiene routine?

- A routine designed to help wind down from a busy day and fall asleep more easily.

- This routine is put in place consistently every night at the same time, so the child knows what to expect. Familiarity and predictability are comforting.

- Here are some tips for a bedtime routine:

Reduce sensory distractions two hours before bedtime	<ul><li>Turn off the television</li><li>Put away all "screens"</li><li>Play quiet games, like board games. No roughhousing.</li><li>Reduce snacks.</li><li>Consider turkey, complex carbohydrates at dinner.</li><li>Chamomile tea can be tasty!</li></ul>
Relax your child	<ul><li>Have them take a warm bath.</li><li>Try a massage; it can be fun and relaxing for your child.</li><li>Use soothing, scented lotions the child finds calming, such as lavender or vanilla.</li><li>Play calming music.</li><li>Initiate a bedtime ritual or prayer.</li></ul>
Prepare for sleep	<ul><li>Draw the curtains and dim the lights.</li><li>Read a story or nursery rhymes in a soft, soothing voice.</li><li>Softly sing lullabies.</li></ul>

It is infinitely easier to start healthy sleep habits early than to try to break unwanted ones later. Adhering to sleep hygiene routines in the early years will pay off when the older child or future adult manages to sleep independently. This goal is worth preparing for!

Chapter 10

Stimulation Needs

"We have got to work on keeping these children
engaged with the world."

— *Temple Grandin, author, speaker, and professor with autism*

We all thrive on stimulation—no one wants to be bored. However, the stimulation needs and challenges of children with ASD are unique. By getting to know your child's personal stimulatory preferences, you can teach self-motivation and self-regulation. The ability to balance the need for stimulation without the risk of becoming overwhelmed is a life skill that will serve them well in their transition to adulthood.

Why does my child need stimulation?

- *Thinking.* For cognitive and sensory enrichment opportunities.

- *Feeling.* To enhance emotional regulation and body-space awareness.

- *Focus.* To help direct and sustain attention.

What kinds of stimulation does my child need?

- *Language stimulation:* Speak in short, simple words or phrases. Narrate what you are doing together. Ham it up and sing often. Many children are musical learners and will remember a song more easily than a spoken narrative. Did any of us memorize the alphabet without first learning the ABC song?

- *Mental stimulation:* Provide developmentally appropriate puzzles or games for independent problem solving. For example, provide some, but not all, of the materials needed for an activity. Let the child figure out what to do.

- *Creative stimulation:* Provide non-directed building opportunities, such as simple blocks or generic Lego pieces with no pattern to follow. Let them build whatever they like and let their imaginations run free.

- *Physical stimulation:* What kid does not enjoy activities such as being lifted high and swung back and forth? That provides stimulation to the vestibular system. You will judge by their reactions how enjoyable that is and whether they want to repeat that positive experience. For some it might be too much, so do not push it if it seems distressing. Families play together in many ways that involve active physical stimulation. One favorite is playing Rowboat: parent and child sit on the floor facing each other, legs out, holding hands. Lean forward and backward as far as you can stretch while singing "Row, Row, Row Your Boat."

What if my child gets overstimulated?

- *Safe haven.* Provide a calm, quiet place to de-stress, far away from the overstimulating experience.

- *Calming touch.* Some children need firm hugs to calm down or a hand on the forehead or shoulder.

- *Space.* Others do not want to be touched at all when overstimulated. Observe and learn your child's preferences, and if they need to be left alone, give them space to calm down on their own.

What kinds of activities result in meltdowns?

- *Observe.* Can you detect your child's early signs of overstimulation? Be a detective and look back at what was going on before your child became overwhelmed.

- *Screens.* Monitor the amount of screen time your child has, including television, tablets, and your phone. When meltdowns occur, review how much screen time they had, and reduce that amount for the next day.

- *Diet.* Limit foods that tend to overstimulate your child. We call those "excitotoxins." They include highly processed foods, food coloring, MSG, and added sugar. Observe whether your child becomes overstimulated after eating these. The solution is obvious!

- *Social.* Some children become overwhelmed being in a crowd, playing with a group of children, or having new people come to the home. Provide a quiet getaway where they can retreat if they need solitude.

- *Tickling.* Many children love to be tickled, but it can be overdone, and the child can go from uncontrolled giggling to uncontrolled sobbing in a moment. Teach your child to take charge of tickling by using tickle games like "Red Light, Green Light." When your child says, "Tickle!" or "Go!" or nonverbally lets you know they want to be tickled, tickle them until they say, "Stop" or "No!" or pull away to tell you nonverbally to stop. As soon as the signal is given, immediately stop all tickling until they say, "Go!" or "Tickle!" or reach out to non-verbally request more. By putting power in their hands, they begin to learn self-advocacy. Be sure that all family members, including the extended family, understand the tickling policy, which they must abide by. Remind them the goal is for the child to know that their body is theirs to control and that adults do not get to touch them without permission, even if it is all in fun. Begin the tickling game with the end in mind: an adult who knows how to self-advocate.

How do I keep their needs in balance?

- **Shelter.** Schedule more calm activities inside the home than social activities outside. For some children with ASD, almost any social activity can be stressful, even if it is a happy event. Many need to rest and recover for twice as long as the social engagement lasted. So, after a one-hour birthday party, you might plan for at least two hours of restful down time with music, books, or a favorite movie.

- **Balance.** Consider alternating physical active play, such as running, biking, or dancing, with still, quiet times, such as reading books or listening to an audio story.

- **Options.** After structured activities such as school or therapy, offer a "choice-board" with pictures of options to choose from, such as coloring, swinging, using clay, putting together a puzzle, running around the backyard, or other activities you know they enjoy. The act of choosing for themselves after a period of compliance can be freeing and balancing. It also paves the way for an adult who knows how to make choices rather than one who always waits for someone else to direct them.

What is stimming?

Stereotypic movements are a variety of repetitive and often uncontrolled movements seen commonly in ASD, but also in children with other neurological disorders, including those with intellectual disabilities. Parents often refer to these stereotypic mannerisms as "stimming" or "stims." These repetitive motions may increase in the presence of anxiety, frustration, boredom, challenges, or stress.

What does stimming look like?

- *Physical stims* include repetitively moving the hands or fingers, flapping elbows, pacing, darting, head or facial movements, and staring.

- *Vocal stims* may include repetitive phrases, throat clearing, coughing, high-pitched squealing, grunting, barking, and echolalia, which is the echoing of words or phrases.

Why do they stim?

- *It's an enigma!* The answer to this question is never clear, but it can be helpful to think about some possible causes.

- **To express emotions.** Some kinds of stimming, such as squealing, fluttering hands, or shaking hands in a "jazz hands" motion, might be a way to express deeply felt joy or excitement. This may or may not be accompanied by a smile or by tilting the face upwards.

- **To communicate distress.** Other kinds of stimming, such as moaning, grunting, waving, flapping the hands, pacing, rocking, or moving in an agitated way, may communicate that something is wrong or that the person is uncomfortable. This may be accompanied by the head being held down, shoulders up, and curling or turning away from others. It appears to be used to help self-regulate emotions or sensory input before it becomes overwhelming.

- **To self-soothe.** Stimming often appears to be comforting to the individuals.

Should I make my child stop stimming?

If a stim is hurting your child or others, such as self-injurious behavior or hitting out at others whether the intent is to hurt them or not, then that behavior should be modified to something safe for everyone. Your BCBA or autism specialist can help find out the function of the harmful stim and substitute another more functional and appropriate behavior that serves the same purpose for your child.

If your child stims to share their joy or excitement when they do not have words to express their emotions, and you try to make them stop, it could send a message that those emotions are somehow wrong or should be covered up. Accept your child's self-expression with joy. Then you may teach further ways of more functional communication, such as saying, "Wow!" or "Oh, boy!" in addition to, but not instead of, their personal form of self-expression.

If your child stims to communicate distress or discomfort, try to find out what is wrong. You may need to become a detective—a true behavior analyst! Put yourself in their shoes and imagine what this moment is like for them. What is going on in the sensory environment? Are there smells, noises, bright lights? What is going on socially? Are there crowds, unfamiliar people or places, unexpected changes or demands? Are they being asked to do a task that they struggle with? Are they trying to avoid a challenging situation? Try to eliminate what you can and provide a calm, quiet place for them to get away. Be grateful that your child was able to use stimming to let you know that your help was needed. If you had focused on making them sit still with "quiet hands," their attempts at communication would have been stifled. When that happens, you can expect their agitated behaviors to escalate rather than go away.

All behaviors have communicative intent. Always listen to the intended communication behind the behavior. The lesson for the child is that when they are feeling out of control and stressed, they will be helped and understood rather than ignored, or worse, punished. When their feelings are honored, it provides the basis for the adult they will become: to learn to control their own emotions and stress.

Your future adult child will be better for having had a childhood where their need for stimulation was honored, and where self-advocacy and self-regulation were encouraged. They may even thank you later!

Chapter 11
The Well-Child Checkup

"The benefits of well-child visits include tracking
your child's ... physical, cognitive, emotional,
and social development."

— *Megan A. Moreno, MD*

Well-child checkups are an important part of caring for any child. Bear in mind, they are children first who just happen to have ASD. New parents often wonder why a well-child checkup is needed if their child is healthy. Be assured that theses checkups are critical for maintaining good health and identifying any potential problems early.

When should I take my child in for well-child checkups?

- **Follow your PCP or pediatrician's guidelines.**

- **The first year** at birth, 3–5 days after birth, 1 month, 2 months, 4 months, 6 months, 9 months, and 12 months of age.

- **The second year** at 18 months and 24 months of age.

- **The third year** at 30 months and 36 months of age.

- **The fourth year** on, continue once a year throughout childhood.

How can I prepare my child?

- *Be positive.* Your own attitude is the most important way your child will learn whether visiting the doctor is a positive experience.

- *Social Stories*™ can be used to explain what might happen in the doctor's office. Books about a child's visit to the doctor are readily available. Better still, make up your own. Creating social stories to pre-learn what might happen can be a wonderful activity.

- *Videos* about a child's visit to the doctor can be found online. Watch the video all the way through to ensure the message is at your child's level and fits within your culture.

How should I prepare for the PCP visit?

- *Do not stress.* Your child will pick up on it.

- *Be comfortable* bringing up your concerns about your child's development.

- *Be prepared* with a list of your greatest concerns so you will not forget while in the office.

- *Prioritize.* You will probably talk to a nurse before the doctor comes in; they may be able to answer some of your questions and tell you which ones are important to ask the doctor.

- *Review* the chart describing what to expect at each age and when to be concerned.

- *Again, do not worry.* If your child is already receiving early intervention services, they will not "fall through the cracks." Your team will help them reach the next developmental level.

- *Schedule a follow-up* if you have more concerns than can be addressed during the appointment. If your doctor prefers, send your additional questions via their email portal.

- *Ask for clarification* if your doctor uses medical jargon or vocabulary you are unfamiliar with. If English is not your first language, ask for an interpreter. Your doctor wants you to fully understand everything that is discussed before you go home.

At every stage of your child's development, keep up with regular well-child checkups. Over time, your doctor will get to know you and your child and can be an invaluable asset to your team. This team will be dedicated to supporting your child in reaching their potential to become happy, healthy adults.

PART IV
Learn to Love the Parade

Get the Most out of Your Team

"Alone we can do so little; together we can do so much."
— *Helen Keller*

Chapter 12

Who Are All
These People?

"For autistic individuals to succeed in this world, they
need to find their strengths and the people that will
help them get to their hopes and dreams."

— *Bill Wong, occupational therapist with autism*

One size does not fit all.

Most agree that children with ASD require extensive and early intervention. Different techniques work well at different ages and stages. A
therapist who is flexible and knowledgeable and who selects the best
techniques is the one you want. Together, establish meaningful and
achievable treatment goals while keeping data on progress and incorporating creative strategies when obstacles arise. Above all, therapy
should be fun!

The Revolving Door of Professionals

When your child starts receiving early intervention services, you
may find a steady stream of teachers, therapists, behavior analysts,
speech pathologists, and occupational therapists coming and going
daily. It can be intimidating. Remember, they are not there to judge
your housekeeping or parenting skills. They are your allies and your

child's support team. They will recommend best practices based on their expertise and experience. Respect their advice and suggestions, and take them to heart. Remember, though, that you are the foremost expert on your child.

If you are not sure about a strategy you are asked to implement with your child, remain open-minded and give it a try. If you find it just will not work in your household, be honest! Do not pretend you are doing the homework when you are not, as it will give a false impression. For example, suppose your child's in-home therapist gives you a stack of flashcards and asks you to review them with your child for thirty minutes a day. Your child screams as soon as you bring out the cards and does not stop until you have put them out of sight. They seem happy enough to work on flashcards with the therapist but strongly protest having you perform the same activity. Tell the teacher about it and give the cards a rest! There are other activities you can do without using those flashcards. Be real about this: if the therapist believes that you have been going over the cards daily when that is not the case, they may form an inaccurate picture of your child's learning ability. Do not try to tell therapists how to do their jobs, but at the same time, do not be intimidated or remain quiet when your insights into how your child learns would be useful to them. You are the captain of the team!

Who are these professionals? Bearing in mind that each child's needs are unique and not everyone will require the same services, here are some that you may have on your child's team.

Behavior Therapists

Your child's team will likely include behavior therapy support staff. Here are some of the people you may meet.

- **BCBA** (Board Certified Behavior Analyst) The BCBA will be involved during the assessment period to help determine your child's needs and eligibility for their services. They may or may not provide direct services to your child, but they will prescribe, supervise, and give guidance to the behavioral team.

- **BCaBA** (Board Certified Assistant Behavior Analyst) The BCaBA may provide in-home services or supervise RBTs, and in turn they may be supervised by the BCBA.

- **RBT** (Registered Behavior Technician) The RBT or behavioral aide provides services as prescribed and supervised by a BCBA or BCABA. They are the people your child will see most often for behavioral intervention services.

Depending on your local service providers, different terms may be used, such as behaviorist, behavior specialist, and behavioral aide. Do not be shy. Ask questions about your behavior professional's philosophies and priorities.

For example, some focus on eliminating stereotypic mannerisms (sometimes referred to a self-stimulatory behaviors), while others recognize stimming as a form of communication, either expressing joy or signaling distress or discomfort. Some strive to achieve strict compliance with directions, while others respond to a child's request to stop an activity, thereby reinforcing self-advocacy.

Some believe that teaching should take place at a table or tray, while others are flexible about working in more natural environments, such as playing on the floor or going outside for a walk. This naturalistic approach is developmentally appropriate and more often greatly beneficial.

Many behavioral therapists seek initially to establish themselves as reinforcers. This entails becoming friends with your child and enjoying fun activities together so your child is happy to see them arrive. Their presence is a more powerful reinforcer than any snack or toy. After this positive relationship is developed, it will be easier for them to steer and guide your child towards completing tasks necessary to support progress.

Services provided by your child's behavioral team will be based on evidence-based best practices. Many people use ABA, IBI, and DTT synonymously. Ask your therapists to explain what is meant by these terms.

- *EI* (Early Intervention) refers to individualized services provided to infants, toddlers, and pre-school-aged children with special needs, including those with ASD.

- *ABA* (Applied Behavior Analysis) applies behavioral principles to real-life situations and environments to teach and reinforce desirable behaviors.

- *IBI* (Intensive Behavior Intervention) usually refers to ABA that is provided one-on-one for 20 or more hours per week. As with ABA and DTT, data is collected to document correct responses and the extent of required prompting.

- **DTT** (Discrete Trial Teaching), as does ABA and IBI, uses the ABC contingency to teach skills. (ABC = Antecedent, what happened before, Behavior, and Consequence, or what happened after.) This is traditionally done at a desk or table but can also be very effective when performed in a naturalistic context.

- **PRT** (Pivotal Response Therapy) is an evidence-based comprehensive service delivery model that utilizes developmental strategies along with ABA principles. It emphasizes learning in the context of naturalistic environments and focuses on core deficits, such as social communication and joint attention. Parents are central, as everyone in the child's environment is engaged in implementing the program.

Speech-Language Pathologist

The Speech-Language Pathologist (SLP) or speech therapist evaluates your child's communication ability. The SLP may directly provide services or indirectly supervise a Speech-Language Assistant. They address both speech (pronouncing sounds and words) and language (putting words together meaningfully), along with social communication and interaction. Many nonverbal children communicate using gestures, facial expressions, signing, and alternative communication devices. It is essential that your child be provided a functional communication system that allows them to express their wants and needs. Clearly, all forms of communication are valuable and should be embraced. Here are some of the tools your SLP may utilize:

- **Speech Therapy** can be provided in group situations or individually. If your child does not yet use words to communicate, your SLP may suggest other methods of communication.

- **PECS** (Picture Exchange Communication System), developed by Andy Bondy and Lori Frost, utilizes picture icons that are exchanged for desired objects to teach preverbal children the power and value of communicating. Children find it easier to offer or exchange a picture of what they want rather than crying and hoping someone will understand. This is not a substitute for oral communication, so do not fear that your SLP is giving up on your child's future verbal capacity by using PECS. Picture exchanges have been shown to lead to and facilitate other forms of communication, including verbal speech.

- **ASL** (American Sign Language). When a very young child wants to communicate but does not yet have words, sign language can be taught to increase communication and decrease frustration. Teaching signs for simple words like eat, drink, and more will start the child down the path of independent communication. This, too, may help facilitate other forms of communication.

- **AAC** (Alternative or Augmentative Communication). This comprises any form of communication other than spoken language, from PECS to ASL to tablets or other electronic devices where pushing a button results in a word or phrase being played. AAC usually refers to a communication system used as an alternative instead of oral language for those who have limited or no spoken language to support or augment their communication. These systems motivate students to communicate, with the benefit of often leading to improved verbal language. It also decreases frustration for a child who knows what they want but cannot convey their needs and ideas.

- *Typing* (keyboarding) can be beneficial to communication. When your child can read but struggles with oral language or written output, becoming facile with typing on a keyboard can a great pragmatic skill. This is an important gift to give their future adult selves!

- *Do not* fall into a habit of helping them find or "facilitating" the correct key by supporting their wrists or guiding them. It is easy for loving adults to over-guide children when typing, not fully cognizant that the words being typed are their own and not their child's. If children are unable to recognize letters and spell words by touching the keys independently, choose another form of communication support. You can return to keyboarding once they are older and have developed improved language and fine motor control.

Occupational Therapists

The OT (Occupational Therapist) addresses the neurodevelopmental deficits a child might have, along with their capacity to regulate sensory information. Functional outcome goals, such as dressing and handwriting, are established, and activities to achieve them are introduced. Sensory integration disorder (SID) and sensory processing disorder (SPD) are conditions where the child's brain and nervous system do not easily process or integrate sensory stimuli. Children may either crave or strongly avoid specific sensory experiences, such as bright lights, loud noises, smells, tastes, textures, touch, movement, or pressure. The OT provides techniques to manage these overwhelming or uncomfortable reactions.

Special Education Teachers

If your child is eligible for special education, an array of services may be offered. These may include enrollment in a developmental preschool classroom, a general education Head Start Program, or a preschool with additional supportive services. These services are laid out in the IEP (Individualized Education Program). If your child is not yet old enough or ready for preschool, an in-home teacher may be provided. Special educators offer a variety of ways to help your child learn.

- *Social Stories*™ were developed by Carol Gray. They are personalized for the child and teach the unwritten strategies and rules needed for self-management in various situations. Social scripts help children learn what to say or do. They may be read aloud to the child to help prepare them for something new, such as a visit to the doctor's office. That is also called pre-learning. They can be used in classrooms and for adults. ASD. The stories are written following a formula that typically includes 2–5 perspective or descriptive sentences and 0–1 directive or control sentences.

- *TEACCH* (The Treatment and Education of Autistic and related Communication-handicapped CHildren) system has helped enhance the quality of life for individuals with ASD and their families across the lifespan. The approach emphasizes visual learning in a structured educational environment and capitalizes on the learner's interests and strengths.

- *Other activities,* including music therapy, movement and dance therapy, and art activities such as drawing, painting, and working with clay or dough, provide wonderful learning opportunities. Yoga provides a sense of peace and relaxation and may help regulate emotions. Support and service animals, including dogs, horses, and even dolphins, increase children's self-confidence and may provide emotional support as well as assistance with a variety of daily living skills. Children, like adults, engage more with others and their environments when they do things they love.

As BCBAs, RBTs, SLPs, OTs and teachers come into your homes and your lives, so, too, will they leave. Service providers may plan to rotate therapists to avail your child of the opportunity to learn from multiple people. Team members may move out of the area or accept different positions. It can be hard to say goodbye to someone you have welcomed into your home and to whom your child has an attachment, but it is all part of the revolving door of services.

Keep working with your child's team. You will remain the constant on the team, the team captain! So, do not give up. The intervention services provided today are the building blocks your adult child will stand on to climb toward their brightest future.

Chapter 13

What Should My Child Be Learning?

"There needs to be a lot more emphasis on what a
child CAN DO instead of what he cannot do."

— *Temple Grandin, author, speaker, and professor with autism*

Now that we have learned about some of the people on your child's
team, we must ask: what should your child be learning? Clearly, it
is important that the goals match your child's need. When choosing
goals, make sure they are SMART: Specific, Measurable, Achievable,
Relevant, and Timely.

- **Specific.** The more specific the goal, the more likely it will be
  achieved. Avoid general, vanilla goals, such as "The child will be
  able to initiate greetings." Instead, be specific, like "Aiden will
  greet his in-home therapist by waving or saying 'Hi' within two
  minutes of the therapist arriving, four out of five days each week."
  Writing "the child" instead of a name sounds like a canned goal,
  rather than an individualized one. Avoid using the phrase "will be
  able to…" when writing goals. A child may be "able to" perform a
  task if they have done it once in their lives, thus they have met the
  goal the same day it was written. Being able to do a task is not the

same as doing it. We want to specifically measure what they do, not what we believe they can do.

- **Measurable.** If our goals are not measurable, we will not know when they have been met. For example, if we write as a goal, Maria will improve her social skills with peers," there is no way to know how this will be measured or whether she has met the goal. Rather, select measurable behaviors that characterize a specific social skill, such as "Maria will remain in a play area for at least two minutes after another child has joined her in that play area rather than exiting immediately, on four out of five opportunities."

- **Achievable.** We want our children to aim high and reach for the stars, but at the same time, we do not want to set them up for failure by setting goals for which they do not have the prerequisite skills. For example, "David will go to the nearest adult and clearly say, 'I need to go to the bathroom,' with enough time to get to the bathroom without accidents," sounds like a fine goal. However, if David has never yet approached an adult for any kind of help, if he cannot yet use words to communicate, and if he does not yet give any indication that he notices or cares whether his diaper is wet or dry, then this goal is unlikely to be achieved in the near future. Goals are not wishes. They must be attainable. If we want David to eventually meet this goal, we must teach him the prerequisite "baby steps." First, he must be taught to self-advocate by asking an adult for help nonverbally, if he is not yet talking. Then, he must be able to communicate his needs, such as by signing "toilet" or pointing to the bathroom. Of course, if he shows no awareness of his diaper being soiled, he may not be developmentally ready for toilet training. Do not stress; he will get there eventually, but do avoid setting unrealistic goals. Think baby steps.

- **Relevant.** Goals should be relevant or meaningful to the child as well as to the adult. This does not mean that we allow the child to set the agenda, but rather, that we need to always ask ourselves if a particular goal is age- and developmentally-appropriate, and whether it potentially benefits the child or just satisfies our desires to see quick progress. Teaching a preschooler to point to a state on a map when given the state bird is not relevant to preschool experience. It would just be a party trick if the child were truly able to do that. Learning what a bird is, looking at picture books about birds, and pointing out birds while on a walk are all age-appropriate. Teaching a child to sit very still without making noise or touching anyone or anything may be a desired goal for adults, but is it truly relevant to what a child needs? Rather, teach taking turns and not interrupting, and to raise a hand rather than call out when they have a question.

- **Timely.** Goals must be time-oriented. This means they should have a clear timeline stated for when the goal should be achieved, whether it is two months, six months, or a year. It also means that it should be timely in relation to the child's development. We do not teach a ten-year-old how to drive a car; we teach children the skills they need to be successful right now. Preschoolers should focus on building with blocks, painting, listening to stories, engaging in pretend play, counting, looking at picture books, taking turns in simple games, or using clay. They are typically not developmentally ready to spend time sitting at a desk, reading, or doing math. Preschool activities might seem childish, but they are child-like. Let us remember that these are young children, and the skills they learn while playing are the building blocks they will use later in life. Let us protect the kingdom of childhood.

What is important for my young child to learn?

- *Functional Communication.* Everyone needs a way to communicate to let others know what they want or need, how they feel, or what they are interested in. If a child is not yet speaking, it does not mean they cannot communicate. In the previous chapter, we discussed alternative ways your child might communicate. It is important to find a communication system that works for your child. This does not mean you are giving up on teaching spoken language. It does mean you are respecting and honoring the child's right to communicate independently in a way that is comfortable for them. (Do not confuse Functional Communication with Facilitated Communication—supported hand-over-hand typing, a highly controversial program which purports to help nonverbal individuals by guiding their hands over a keyboard to spell words.)

- *Basic Self-Help Skills.* We want our children to become independent adults, and this means teaching them basic self-help skills as soon as they are developmentally ready. These include toileting, feeding, dressing, washing hands, brushing teeth, bathing, and other tasks we expect them to be able to do as adults. It is possible to teach many children with ASD subjects that might be considered above their age level, such as reading multisyllabic sight words on flashcards, but their future teachers will not be impressed by their advanced reading ability or any other splinter skill if they are not yet fully toilet-trained or able to communicate socially with peers. Of course, if they are fascinated by reading and memorizing facts, allow them to pursue those interests. When the time comes to write goals, though, focus on the skills that will be important throughout their lifetime.

- **Visual Schedules.** Nearly all of us use some type of visual schedule such as calendars or smartphones that help organize our lives. Children with ASD benefit from structure, and having a visual schedule is most helpful. A repeated routine is comforting. Create picture schedules for different parts of your child's day, such as morning routines, getting ready for school, toileting, washing hands, mealtimes, and bedtime schedules. Visual schedules have been popularized by the TEACCH program, described above. Create your own by laminating charts with two columns of hook-and-loop fasteners. The left column, "To Do," should have small picture icons of the steps in a schedule, affixed with a hook-and-loop fastener on the back. Once each step is completed, the picture is moved to the right column, "Done." Having a clear visual image of what to do next, what to expect, and when they are done, is helpful in developing self-regulation and self-management capacities.

Work with your team to develop SMART goals for your child that focus on functional communication, basic self-help skills, and learning to follow visual schedules to keep your child moving forward with the skills they will need as adults.

Chapter 14

What Shouldn't My Child Be Learning?

"Why should I cry for not being an apple, when I was born an orange? I'd be crying for an illusion. I may as well cry for not being a horse."

— *Donna Williams, author with autism*

Earlier, we discussed what your child should be learning. This changes at every age and stage and in relation to each child's unique strengths and needs.

What about things your child should not learn? There are a few. While learning to comply with adult instructions is important for safety and for learning, teaching unconditional compliance can be dangerous. Be careful not to instill the idea that your child must comply with whatever an adult tells them to do, regardless of whether it feels wrong to them. This is an invitation to potential abuse.

Do Not Teach Unconditional Compliance

- *Teach a child when to say "no."* All humans have rights. Avoid letting your child believe that rights end when teaching begins. Give them appropriate ways to protest things they do not like.

- **Listen to them.** Children communicate with their behavior. When they are uncomfortable or unhappy, try to determine why. Screaming during a lesson could be due to pain from an earache. They may get up from a chair because they need to have a bowel movement. They may be bothered by a therapist's perfume or coffee breath or just be bored by pointing to another round of picture cards. Behavior always has a communicative intent. First, rule out medical reasons for unusual behaviors. Your child's doctor can help ensure there are no underlying physical causes of the behavior.

- **Let them know you understand.** If you cannot ascertain an obvious reason for the protest other than that the child simply refuses to comply, provide language for their protest. Tell them "I know; you don't like this."

- **Help them verbalize their protest.** If they can speak, give them the words you believe their behavior is communicating. "Say, 'No, thank you,' or "Tell me, 'Break, please.'"

- **Honor their voice.** When they say or nonverbally communicate "No, thank you," immediately switch to a different learning activity. When they say "Break, please," provide a brief break right away. This emphasizes the power of communication. It may feel as if it will slow down learning, but there is a more important lesson to be learned. They are learning that they have a voice and that they are worthy of respect.

- **Return to teaching.** Although we respect every child's voice and preferences, it does not follow that instructions go out the window because a child would rather watch cartoons than work.

Especially when children are very young, learning can continue on the carpet instead of at a table, but regardless, instruction continues. We know that the more naturalistic the environment, the more children learn. Listening and respecting the child's preferences helps prepare them to become adults who can self-advocate. Continuing with instruction after acknowledging the protest helps prepare children to work with future teachers and supervisors in the workplace.

Do Not Teach Dog-and-Pony Show Tricks

- *Cut down on cutesy posts.* Some children are natural mimics and can imitate anything you model. What can be fun and cute now may not be so funny when they are teens and adults. Respect the privacy of your future child by being careful with what you post.

- *Refrain from rage posts.* It may be tempting to post videos of another lengthy meltdown out of frustration. You may be looking for support or just to vent, but be cautious and do not give in to this temptation. That video you upload to the internet lives on forever. Just don't!

Do Not Teach Calculus before Communication

- *Academics are easier.* Regardless of how impressive learning calculus is for a preschooler, it is not nearly as important as functional communication. If a child has an intense interest in calculus or any other advanced subject, let them pursue it as a hobby, but it should not take precedence over social communication goals and basic life skills.

- *What is important to learn is difficult to teach.* Teach it anyway. While it is easier to learn the alphabet than toileting or self-regulation, you decide which skills are important prerequisites to future success.

Are Children the Center of the Universe or Not?

- *Sometimes it is all about them.* There will be times when you want to enter a child's world and spend time following their leads. Consider the Greenspan Floortime Approach, or Relationship Development Intervention (RDI). You might call it "Tina Time." The only rule for "Tina Time" is that Tina gets to decide what you will do, within safety limitations, of course. If she is looking at shadows, you look at shadows. If she is spinning in a circle, you spin too. During "Tina Time," you do not try to redirect her; just enjoy what she enjoys. She learns that her interests are valid, an important part of developing self-esteem that will strengthen her future adult self.

- *Sometimes it is not about them.* Most of the time is not "Tina Time." When you are on the way to a doctor's appointment, you cannot spend an hour watching water from a neighbor's sprinkler run down the gutter. Learning that there are times when adults call the shots is an important life lesson that will help your future adult child get along with colleagues and authority figures.

Maintain a balance of teaching important life skills while refraining from teaching skills that are simply not germane; this is a worthy undertaking. Your adult child may not actually thank you later, but their future success will reflect the time you spent on life's valuable lessons during their formative years.

PART V
Out and About

Venturing Forth into
the Community

"Not all classrooms have four walls."

— Anonymous

Chapter 15

The Unwritten Rules of the Park and Playground

"A trip to the playground is like having a playdate with
whoever shows up. Unless everyone agrees to a few
ground rules, things can quickly devolve ..."

— *Jerry Mahoney, dad and blogger*

There are unwritten rules to bringing children to a public park. For instance, precious toys that your child cannot fall asleep without should be left home or in the car. Parents are expected to police their own child but not to point out when others are not following rules. Young children may walk unaware in front of a moving swing or try to climb up a slide when another child is about to slide down. To keep your child from harm, supervise to the extent necessary for safety without hovering. But what about children's unwritten playground rules? Is your child with ASD even aware of those rules?

What do the other kids know that mine does not?

- *Kids know how to take turns.* Most children have learned to wait their turn for the swing or slide. If your child is unaware that others are waiting, they may go straight to the front of the line. That is where pre-learning comes in. Prepare them in advance by discussing waiting in lines and looking for lines at the equipment. If you know they love to slide, point to the line and say, "There is where you can line up to slide."

- **Kids know how to ask.** Most verbal children have learned to ask permission before acting; "Can I play?" or "Can I use that?" If your child is unable to communicate what they want, they might charge right into a game in progress or grab another's toy. Practice, at home, playing with a toy they like, and encourage them to ask for it either verbally or nonverbally. As soon as they gesture or say, "My turn?" give them the toy for a while. If they grab the toy, put it up on a shelf for a short period (the toy is on Time Out, not the child) and then try again. Model the behavior you want them to use. Consider bringing siblings into the act.

- **Kids know how to make friendly overtures.** For younger children, simply looking at another child sharing the sand box and smiling is the extent of social initiation. Older children comment about what they are doing together or compliment others. "Did you see that?" "That was cool!" or "I like your backpack." When kids with ASD are unaware or not yet able to engage in age-appropriate outreach, others may assume they are irritating, unfriendly, or rude. Others might choose to avoid them.

What will the other parents think of me if my child seems different?

- *It does not matter what they think.* Every child and every parent is different. Other parents do not know your child's challenges. What they think about you is none of your business.

- *Should you share the diagnosis?* Maybe. If you will be interacting with the same families regularly, you may choose to disclose your child's diagnosis to help them understand. Autism Society of America (ASA) has printed cards explaining the diagnosis for such situations. But if you just happen to be sharing a swing-set with a family you probably will not see again, there is no reason to share private information.

- *Should you drop hints?* Some parents wear T-shirts with autism-positive messages to subtly educate others. If people understand, they may give a child the benefit of the doubt if atypical behaviors become apparent.

- *Should you keep it to yourself?* Others choose to keep the diagnosis private. This should not be out of shame or embarrassment about ASD, but to protect a child's privacy. Once older, they can decide for themselves any needed disclosures. If you feel something should be said in a situation, make general comments, such as "He is not much of a talker yet and still learning social skills, but he does enjoy playing near other kids" or "She loves swinging so much it's hard for her to learn to take turns, but we're working on it."

How can I keep my child safe?

- *Reconnaissance.* Scout the park in advance. Is it properly fenced, or could a child make a break and run to the street unhindered? Is there sufficient playground equipment, such as swing sets, slides, or bouncy horses, so wait times will be short? Check restrooms for cleanliness, and bring your own soap and paper towels just in case. Make the restroom the first stop once you arrive to familiarize your child for later when they really need it.

- *Vigilance.* Refrain from checking your phone for emails or social media. If you chat with a friend, do so while scanning the area so you always know your child's whereabouts. It only takes a moment for a child to disappear.

- *Flexibility.* Always have a Plan B in your back pocket. You may have packed a lunch and planned for a two-hour afternoon at the park, but if your child becomes overstimulated by sensory or social overload, be ready to scrap the plan and head home. Do not err by trying to extend your stay beyond the point when your child can self-regulate, as a meltdown is bound to ensue. If a sibling would have loved to stay longer, it seems unfair to leave early, so plan something special for Plan B once you get home. Spread out a blanket and have your picnic on the floor with a favorite movie. Let the sibling choose an activity for the family, such as making ice cream sundaes or popping corn. That will help take the sting out of the change of plans.

Although there are many things to consider and plan for when you and your child venture forth into the community, the experiences gained will be worth the effort. By helping your child expand their horizons now, you are preparing them for exciting future experiences out and about in the world.

Chapter 16

How to Go to the Grocery Store without Going Crazy

> "Given the right conditions, taking toddlers and preschoolers to the supermarket can be productive, educational, and dare we say it—fun."
>
> — *Elizabeth M. Ward, MS, RD*

It was once so easy to take your baby to the grocery store, sleeping safely in their infant seat or seat-belted in the cart seat when they were old enough to sit up. But that honeymoon is over! Babies grow up, and that trip to the grocery store is not nearly so simple anymore.

You have probably seen parents struggle with children screaming for a toy at the top of their lungs. The parents give in, buying a few minutes of peace and quiet. Unfortunately, it does not stop there, for they are soon begging for something else. If begging does not work this time, they may up the ante and begin to whine and progress to screaming. You and the rest of the shoppers move away to a quieter part of the store, but those poor parents are living it! Might they have reinforced begging and screaming by giving the child what they begged for? If they give in again, will they have reinforced screaming?

You may also have seen parents hand their child a lollipop as they enter the store, with the proviso that they be on their best behavior for the entire trip. We all know such contracts will likely dissolve as quickly as the lollipop: when the candy is gone, the begging, whining, and screaming begin.

You can have a different experience if you look at the interaction from a behavioral perspective. Stimulus leads to a response, which can lead to the original stimulus either recurring more frequently in the future or decreasing in frequency. In the moment, the parents got what they wanted—some peace and quiet—by giving in. But what about the long term? If the stimulus is the child screaming and the response is the parent giving in, the likelihood is that the child will scream again whenever they want something, because it worked!

So, what can you do instead? Look at the situation, not only from your own perspective, but also from your child's point of view. Then plan a strategy to avoid potential problems.

The Parents' Perspective

- *Necessity.* Buying groceries is a necessity, and it is not always possible to go without your child. You need to find a way to make the experience positive for everyone.

- *Opportunity.* Parents know that every outing provides an opportunity for learning. A trip to the store can become a lesson in following a list or learning about nutrition, money, and the holy grail: delayed gratification! Unfortunately, these opportunities are lost if your child is screaming and trying to climb out of the shopping cart. Let us look at it from the child's perspective.

Through a Child's Eyes

- *Sensory Overload.* A child with ASD may be overwhelmed by high-echoing ceilings, bright, flickering lights, colorful displays, or the uncomfortable wire-cart seat. These alone can cause a sensory meltdown.

- *Social Overload.* Grocery stores are surprisingly social places. Other children, shoppers, and especially store clerks will often try to engage your child in social conversation, which can be stressful and confusing. Crowds of people in unfamiliar places can cause a social meltdown.

- *Expectation Overload.* If your child expects a short trip or that you were only going to one store, but you must make other stops, stressful responses are likely. Also, if a very young child sees a toy on the shelf identical to one they have at home, they may believe it is theirs and thus expect to take it home where it belongs. Thwarted expectations can lead to meltdowns.

- *Time Overload.* The sights, sounds, and people at the grocery store may be thrilling rather than overwhelming for a time, and your child may seem quite happy to be there. Until they are not. No matter how much fun it was at first, when it goes on too long, a meltdown is in the cards!

Strategies: Set Them Up for Success.

- *Sensory Strategies.* Consider using headphones for listening to favorite tunes, a broad-brimmed hat or hood they can hide in to keep out bright light, and a padded seat cover for the cart. If children are bothered by smells in the detergent aisle, bring a small stuffed toy sprayed with a favorite scent, such as vanilla or rose water. When chemical smells become bothersome, they can hug the toy to inhale a more soothing aroma.

- *Social Strategies.* Children are less bothered by the stressful social whirlwind going on around them if they have something to focus on. Consider packing a supermarket bag with books, snacks, or toys to only bring out when they are in the cart, so that they appear special. Make sure you do not include items for sale in the store you are in, to avoid being charged! Precious toys may wear a leash or ribbon tied to the cart handle for quick retrieval if dropped.

- *Time Limiting Strategies.* Have a list, have a plan, get in and get out. Older children can help by picking up certain items on the list. If you have the luxury of shopping with another adult, divide the list by area and take two carts. The shorter the trip, the easier it will be on your child.

Reinforcement: Pay the Piper.

- *Choose your Reward.* We all expect to be paid when we work, so it is not spoiling your child if you offer a reinforcement to show your appreciation for their cooperation. Make it something enjoyable but not so expensive that you cannot repeat the same reward on each trip to the store. Children with ASD often have a strong attachment to predictability, so begin the way you would choose to continue. Some parents allow a small piece of candy at the end of every trip to the store but limit candy at other times. Others prefer to avoid food rewards and offer extra screen time instead. Rather than buying a parade of small, cheap toys which will be soon broken, consider buying yourself a big-ticket item you know your child will enjoy over time, such as a video game system. We suggest you buy it for yourself rather than for them, and make this clear, so you can keep it on a high shelf in your room most of the time. When they have earned time to play with your game, only then bring it out for the agreed-upon amount of time they earned, then put it away again until the next trip. Older children usually respond to this kind of reward, while younger children may need something more immediate, such as that special snack or treat.

- *Choose your Time.* When do you give the reward? That depends on the reward. Older children working to earn time on your video game can wait until they get home. For younger children who may have a piece of candy, consider a two-part agreement. First, they agree to stay in the cart (or walk beside it) using their indoor voices until check-out time. If they comply, they may choose one candy from a limited field of two or three choices the parent is willing to buy. The candy must then be put on the belt, scanned, paid for, and bagged. The second part of the agreement is that they cooperate with being buckled into the car seats. Now they can get their treat!

- *Don't sweat the small stuff.* We have heard "Choose your battles" more times than we can count. Not everything is equally important. If your child has stayed safe and kind at the store without climbing out or shouting, that may be good enough. Later, they can learn to answer when the clerk tries to initiate a conversation. For now, cut your kid some slack. That is not your battle for today.

It is not easy to plan a trip to the supermarket with care and attention to detail, but it can save your sanity. Remember, the more advance planning, the greater your chances of success. As your child learns what is expected, and the more you set them up for success, a trip to the grocery store can become the fun and educational opportunity you always hoped it could be.

Chapter 17

Navigating Barber Shops, Dentists' Offices, and the Rest of the World

"On the surface, a sheltered life spent on your
favourite activities might look like paradise, but I
believe that unless you come into contact with some
of the hardships other people endure, your own
personal development will be impaired."

— *Naoki Higashida, author with autism at age 15*

While it is certainly easier to leave a child at home to happily engage
in favorite activities, this is not always possible, and indeed, as Naoki
Higashida has written, remaining in that paradise can detract from social development. Some outings are optional; you can cut your child's
hair at home to avoid barber shops and find a sitter when you need to
go to the DMV. Other outings require your child's attendance, most
notably medical and dental appointments. These excursions can be
quite challenging for your child and for you. So, how can you smooth
the way to ensure a more positive experience? Planning is key.

What should I do before my child's appointment?

- *Several weeks before...* Make at least one advance trip to the office or barber shop your child will visit. Call ahead to let them know you would like to enlist their help in allowing your child to familiarize themselves with the new environment. Explain how this will ensure a more successful appointment. Ask permission to photograph, or even video, staff members the child may encounter. On your reconnaissance mission, take photos of the building from the outside of the office entrance, especially if you can get one of your child smiling by the door. (Do not beg for a smile, but rather try saying something silly to elicit natural giggles!) Go inside and get shots of the waiting room, the toys or books on shelves, and the smiling staff members at the desk. Take photos from the child's eye level; they will relate better that way. If possible, get a photo of your child sitting on the exam table or in the dentist's or barber shop's chair. Another big smile would be great! Watch for signs of fatigue or sensory overload. Before your child starts to fuss, call it a day and leave quickly. A trip to a favorite place for a special treat will now be in order. Be sure to photograph your child having fun here as well.

- *Several days before...* Your child can now enjoy looking at these pictures on an electronic device or printed in a binder. Plastic sheet protectors are a good idea, but if your child loves them, consider creating a permanent book online. The idea is to have a series of photos, from the parking lot to the front door to the waiting room, front desk, and finally the exam room, followed, of course, by the post-appointment treat. Show the staff members smiling. Include pictures of your child looking happy. Review the video or booklet several times, right up to the day of the appointment. If your child resists when you try to read it to them, just leave it around where they can pick it up themselves on their own time. Avoid cajoling, but make it accessible to increase the likelihood that they will look at it.

- *The night before...* Read the book as a bedtime story. Remind them of the fun they had enjoying their post-visit treat.

What should I do on the day of my child's appointment?

- *Start on a positive note.* That starts with you! Your child will pick up on any unspoken stress. Model a positive demeanor. Now's the time for deep breathing or yoga.

- *Review your story and pictures.* Remind your child where you will go right after their appointment.

- *Arrive early enough...* They may want to check out the toys in the waiting room or take a few minutes to get used to being in the office before transitioning to the exam room.

- *...But not too early.* You do not want boredom or your child asking to leave. Bring the book or video to look at. Have a "bag of tricks" ready, including fun toys, treats, or their favorite movie on your phone to keep them engaged.

- *What about accommodations?* A favorite toy can be brought into the appointment with your child, and the professional can pretend to give the toy a haircut, listen to the toy's heart, or check the toy's teeth. At the dentist's office, if pressure or weight helps your child relax, request that they leave the leaded apron on if your child enjoys it. It can act as a calming weighted blanket for those who crave deep proprioceptive pressure.

- *Advocate.* If your child is struggling, you may be offered restraints to allow the doctor's examination or treatment to be carried out. Remember, you are your child's advocate and their voice when they cannot speak for themselves. If your child loves to be bundled and calms down when wrapped like a burrito, they may respond positively to certain restraints. However, if you believe that the restraints will be overly upsetting or traumatizing for your child, step in and speak up. In certain situations, invasive procedures can be performed under mild sedation or general anesthesia. Check with your doctor about safe alternatives.

What about after the appointment?

- *Fast getaway.* Avoid small talk with the staff on your way out the door. Remind your child of the fun place you are going next. This is their reinforcement. Let the staff know you will call back to schedule the next appointment. Try and prepay by phone before the visit.

- *Prompt reinforcement.* Go directly to the happy place (or provide the reward if it is an item). This is not the time to work on delayed gratification.

- *Review later.* Go over the book that night if they had a positive experience, commenting on the parts you believe they liked best, including the reinforcement after the appointment.

What if something goes wrong?

- *Plan B.* Always have a Plan B. If your child becomes overwhelmed and a meltdown ensues, it is not a failure to try again another day. If they do not complete the appointment, do not provide the promised reward. Be upbeat and let them know they can try again in the future.

- *Exit strategy.* Park nearby and be prepared to carry your child to the car during a meltdown to provide privacy and a quiet place to return to a balanced state. Give them time. Be calm and carry on! It will not help to berate your child or feel at fault for a sensory or social meltdown, which is out of anyone's control.

- *Try, try again.* Make another appointment and go through the previous steps. If you see where Plan A went awry, adjust. There is no one right way to manage appointments, and every plan should be individualized to your child's needs.

The more you plan, the easier it will be for your child to go new places and interact with new people. For future appointments, review the booklet or the video. It will become easier over time, and who knows? Perhaps the day will come when your child will look forward to appointments ... or at least participate with good humor to earn the reward.

Chapter 18

Safety First ...
But What if They Get
Lost Anyway?
Prepare First Responders
to Find Your Child

"Perhaps the most predictable law enforcement and public safety contact will be when less independent autistic children, adolescents and adults are reported missing. Their limited self-help skills increase the danger and urgency of search and rescue operations."

— *Dennis Debbaudt*

A parent's worst nightmare! A child gets lost, and it happens all too often. Many children with ASD love to run or climb or shut themselves up into cozy, tight spaces. It is quite common for them to run or wander away from caregivers or secure locations. Even verbal children may fail to respond when their name is called. This is called "elopement," clearly a traumatic situation for a child and caregivers alike.

So, what to do? When a lost child is not found quickly enough, call first responders immediately. Prevention comes first, but when your child's sense of adventure outruns your best-laid plans, help is available. As with any behavior, it is important to understand the reason or communicative intent for elopement. What might they be trying to tell us, or is it simply wanderlust? Alternative behaviors and communication need to be taught. Prevention comes first.

Prevention Tips

- *Safety rules.* Create an emergency plan. Teach safety rules and review them before every outing. Consider making a book, a pictorial list, or a video of your child repeating the rules. Some good rules include: Stay with the family. Hold a grownup's hand. Stay away from strangers. Ask if you need the restroom; do not just go by yourself. Whatever the rules are, make sure everyone understands them.

- *Safety aids.* Medical alert bracelets can inform first responders that the child has ASD and may not be able to respond verbally. If the child is nonverbal or becomes nonverbal when under stress, having printed cards is useful. In crowded places, such as the mall, or potentially dangerous locations, such as the beach or a lake, a harness, backpack, or life jacket with a cord attached might be used. A hand-holding rule is great, but if a child pulls away and takes off running, this can be risky. A small child who adores water play but does not yet swim and a large body of water is a dangerous combination. They may feel compelled to run into the water they love so much, unaware of the depth or waves. If your child is one whose safety depends on wearing a harness, do not be dissuaded by well-meaning but uninformed folk who berate you for having a child "on a leash." Better to be tethered to a parent and safe than lost or injured.

- **Safety tips.** As you exit your home, take a picture of your child. This can go into a scrapbook or memory album later, but having a photo of your child standing alone is something you can share with the first responders. They will ask for a physical description, picture, and what they were wearing. The baby picture in your wallet will not be useful, and it can be difficult to remember what they were wearing when you are inwardly panicking.

When to call 911.

- **Immediately.** When a child is lost, there is no 24-hour waiting period before reporting them missing. It is important to get professionals involved.

What to do while waiting for first responders.

- **Be ready.** Make sure someone is available to flag down the first responders when they arrive.

- **Be calm.** This is difficult. Take slow, steady breaths, breathing in through your nose and out through your mouth. Stay focused on the now and what you can do to help rather than letting your mind race toward some dreaded future catastrophe.

- **Keep searching.** Your search does not end while you await the first responders. Better to be embarrassed that you found the child before they arrive than to wait. Time is crucial.

Where to search.

- **At home,** search closets, piles of laundry, under beds, inside cupboards, vehicles, and appliances, and in any tight space a child could fit.

- **Out and about,** look in restrooms, trash bins, cardboard boxes, up trees, in bushes, and clothing racks in stores. It is surprising how small a space a child can fit themselves into.

- **Use their interests.** If they love trains or swinging or buses or water or nature, go to nearby places where they might seek these things. A special interest or passion, such as vehicles or animals, may provide helpful clues. Searchers may even sing the child's favorite song or play a tape with the opening music from their favorite show. Familiar music can bring a frightened child out of hiding.

What to do to help first responders.

- **Be controlled.** Use slow, deep breathing to keep yourself calm enough to communicate.

- **Be clear.** When asked a question, stop and think so you can give a clear, concise answer. Your mindful breathing will help clear your thoughts so you can answer questions and provide the information officers need. Your calmness and clarity will be your anchor, along with the knowledge and conviction that most lost children are found unharmed and returned to their parents in a short time.

- **Be courageous.** There is nothing more frightening for a parent than losing a child. Find your inner strength and remind yourself that professionals know how to find your child. You will get through this.

What not to do.

- **Do not panic.** Keep breathing.

- **Do not lose hope.** Remember: 97% of missing children are found, usually within hours.

- **Do not place blame.** Blaming yourself or others is pointless and damaging.

When it is all over.

- **Hug your child.** And then hug them again.

- **Thank your first responders.** These helpers go above and beyond.

- **Go home.** Everyone is exhausted. Time for some self-care and recovery.

Tragedies are rare, and most lost children are quickly and easily reunited with their parents, often with little realization of the turmoil they have caused. Do not worry needlessly about things which might happen in the future, but be prepared to act quickly and calmly should the need arise. The key is prevention. Prepare now to avoid any future emergency situations.

PART VI
Emotional
Roller Coaster

When There is No Emoji to Express How They Feel

"The finest emotion of which we are capable is the mystic emotion. Herein lies the germ of all art and all true science."

— *Albert Einstein*

Chapter 19

* *

Negative Feelings: Anxiety, Anger, Sadness

"We cry, we scream, we hit out and break things.
But still, we don't want you to give up on us.
Please keep battling alongside us."

— *Naoki Higashida, author with autism at age 15*

Parents feel their children's pain when they are overcome by anxiety, anger, or sadness. It is that much more difficult when a child is nonverbal or when a verbal child loses the ability to use words in the throes of extreme emotion. A child's behavior is a mode of communication. What are they trying to tell us? Use your own communication abilities to help your child express themselves. Slow down, simplify your words, and model what you believe they are feeling. "You feel mad that your toy broke." "You feel sad that Grandma can't visit us." "You feel afraid of the loud garbage truck outside."

After identifying their feelings, follow up with suggestions of what they can do. "We can try to fix the toy." "We can draw a picture for Grandma and call her on the phone." "We can play music and watch the garbage truck from the window to see it go away."

Mindfulness strategies can help a child cope with anxiety and anger. "Let's take a few deep breaths." Try to predict the triggers that might overwhelm or overload your child, and endeavor to either avoid the aversive experience or prepare for it.

Here are some specific tips for riding the meltdown roller coaster!

How can I help my child cope with anxiety?

- *"I feel..."* Encourage children to find a word to express their feeling.

- *Accept.* Avoid saying "There is nothing to be afraid of" or in any way deny what they are feeling. This diminishes the capacity for self-expression, robs them of a voice, and takes away the right to own and honor their emotions. Validate feelings!

- *Reframe.* Is there a different phrase that implies the same sentiment but feels better? Instead of saying "This is scary," try substituting "This is an adventure." Include your child in this reframing discussion so that they own it and do not feel that their words are dismissed with your substitutions.

- *Measure.* Have them identify the extent or level of anxiety on a picture thermometer scale ranging from blue (calm) to yellow (nervous) to orange (pretty anxious) to red (super anxious).

- *"I can..."* Help your child choose a coping strategy that matches the level of anxiety. At blue, no strategy is needed because everything is okay. At yellow, encourage deep breathing and reframing, describing the situation in a more positive light. At orange, ask the child to close their eyes and picture a calm, relaxing place where they can practice muscle relaxation techniques by tensing and relaxing various body parts. At red, request help from a grownup and leave the area to a safe, quiet place if necessary.

- *Breathe.* Slow, deep breaths, in through the nose and out through the mouth, help reduce anxiety.

How can I help my child manage anger?

- *Breathe...I feel...Accept...Reframe...I can...* The mindfulness strategies for anxiety are also helpful for anger.

- *Stoplight.* Imagine a stoplight. When the light is green, every-thing is good to go. When irritation or annoyance begins to grow, the light turns yellow. It is time to slow down, be cautious, and practice mindful breathing and relaxation strategies. The red light happens when anger keeps growing. This is when your child needs to take a step or two back from the person or situation and may-be take a shower or lie in bed. Folding hands under crossed arms keeps everyone safe. Your child should be taught to ask for help once they reach this stage.

How can I help my child express and deal with sadness?

- *Accept.* Do not ignore sad things that happen in life or try to cover up sad feelings.

- *Acknowledge* your child's feelings, even though it might seem triv-ial. To them it is very real.

- *Be there.* Sometimes, remembering sad events from the past brings about the same intensity of response it did at the time, and there might be a need to cry about it before moving on. Children need to know you are still there for them.

- **Offer a hug.** Hold them, but respect boundaries if they do not want to be touched.

- **Safety.** Create a quiet place to safely experience their emotions.

- **Creativity.** For older children who are able, allow the opportunity to draw or write about feelings, with no censorship.

All humans experience emotion, and we each do so in our own way. Unconditional love is a valuable gift we can give our children. We demonstrate this by acknowledging big feelings without minimizing them, however intense, out of proportion, or inexplicable they might seem to us. Standing alongside a child as they struggle with emotional expression is an act of unconditional love.

Chapter 20

Positive Feelings: Joy, Delight, Ecstasy

(Even the happy emotions can be overwhelming.)

"My autism makes things shine... Playing the piano makes me very happy. Playing Beethoven is like your feelings—all of them—exploding."

— *Mikey Allcock, teen poet, pianist, artist, altruist with autism*

Many people with ASD feel emotions intensely, including the positive ones. Many find great joy in experiences such as watching dust motes drift in sunbeams or water cascading over their hands. Some experience intense delight in learning something new related to their passions, such as discovering a new dinosaur or planet. The happiness they feel at these times may far exceed what most of us experience. What a gift it is to find ecstasy in the everyday!

Social events, beloved by many, may prove too much for them. A highly anticipated birthday party may culminate in the birthday child retreating to a place far from the crowd. We may worry unduly that they are having a terrible time, but the reverse may be true. They may be delighted with the idea of the party but prefer to enjoy it from a distance. If you cajole them to stay in the party, feelings may build up to a meltdown. This does not mean we should deny them birthday parties, but if a child can communicate, we should ask about their preferences. Would they prefer to go to a park where they could swing alone while the others play party games? Would they prefer a family-only party or a trip to a museum, observatory, aquarium, or zoo? If your child cannot express themselves, you know your child. When are they happiest? What makes them smile and laugh? Perhaps an ideal birthday is watching a favorite cartoon over and over and eating chicken nuggets and fries. Perhaps it is riding a train, going to a LEGO® store, or taking a tree-hugging trip to a park. Let us not impose our notions of what a birthday party should be; instead, let the child lead the way and call the shots!

Preparing for joy.

- *Accept* their preferences. Do not judge what makes someone happy. Follow their lead.

- *Anticipate* the likelihood of a child becoming overwhelmed by the depth of their emotions when face-to-face with something they love. Seeing live penguins rather than just reading or watching videos about them can be an overwhelming emotional experience, even for someone for whom penguins are a passion.

- *Empower* them. Remember the tickling STOP-GO game. They may be delighted to be tickled, but too much can readily cross to tears. Let your child request tickles and give breaks between tickling sessions to catch their breath and maintain emotional equilibrium.

The same rule applies to any fun, active game that can become overwhelming, such as being swung high or playing chase games. Have fun, but practice moderation.

- **_Be patient._** Allow your child time at a favorite exhibit to explore at their own speed. Have your spouse take the siblings to the rest of the museum or other attractions. Your child with ASD may be happiest to spend the entire zoo trip at the flamingo lagoon or the whole aquarium visit with the jellyfish. Do not exhort them to see and do everything, as that could lead to becoming overwhelmed and melting down.

Rejoice with your child when they are blissfully, ecstatically happy, and be there for them if these emotions get out of control and become more difficult to manage. Adults with autism have shared that the intense joy felt when engaged in passionate interests is something they would not trade for the world. Indeed, some report sympathy for "neurotypicals," whose feelings appear to be tame and tempered compared to the bliss of autism. Let us celebrate the exhilaration of the multitude of wonders in life—through our children's eyes.

Chapter 21

Strategies for Dealing with Overstimulation

"The monotony and solitude of a quiet life stimulates the creative mind."

— Albert Einstein

What if an event, outing, or experience gets out of hand and your child becomes overstimulated or overcome by emotions? This is inevitable and will happen despite a parent's best efforts to maintain balance. So, do not sweat the small stuff! It is nothing personal. It is just business as usual! Rather, take steps to allow your child to regain equilibrium. Remember, they are not their behavior. A sensory or social overload-induced meltdown is not a manipulative tantrum. Children are not trying to get at us. They do not like meltdowns any more than we do, and while outbursts cannot always be prevented, we can help alleviate the situation.

Change the people.

- *A crowd.* If a meltdown occurs in a crowded place, remove your child to a more isolated location. No one wants an audience when out of control.

- *A bully.* You may not believe that a cousin or friend is a bully, and they may not be actually bullying your child at all. However, if your child feels pressured to participate in games they do not want to play, or if they interpret playful banter as hurtful insults, they may be experiencing bullying. Give them an out if they do not want to be around the children who they feel are bullying them. Listen without minimizing concerns when a child reports bullying behaviors. Children need to know that we will always pay attention to their concerns and that we will protect them and help extricate them from such situations. On the other hand, if you are sure that the playful bantering or joking was directed equally towards all peers and did not specifically target your child, it may be useful to share that insight about the nature of kidding around, and, of course, the cardinal rule of teasing. Whoever loses their cool first loses the game! Since your child might have difficulty processing social emotional situations, they may need guidance on how to handle them.

Change the place.

- *Volume.* If you are in a building with piped-in music, high ceilings that echo voices, applause and cheering, or tennis shoes squeaking on a gym floor, your child's auditory sense might be under assault. Your child might cover their ears or head. Provide an escape to a quiet place, or offer headphones.

- *Visual.* If the room is visually distracting, with bright, flashing, or twinkling lights and brightly colored carpet or tiles, your child's visual system may become overwhelmed. Wearing dark glasses may help, but if not, you may need to leave the area.

Change the plan.

- *Plan B.* Always have a Plan B in your back pocket for when a child needs to get out of a situation. Let the family know in advance what that will be, so you can execute Plan B quickly and with minimal disruption. A pre-arranged secret signal can alert everyone to your intention.

- *Exit strategy.* Know where the exits are to be able to leave quickly and easily. Make sure the rest of the family or party knows where you will go if you need to get out.

You have the power to make changes to your child's environment to allow them to relax, breathe, and gradually return to a feeling of harmony. This will most likely take longer than you envision, but it cannot be rushed. Helping children find a safe place to process feelings of sensory or social overload is a gift that yields future rewards. A child will feel more confident in going out and trying new things when they have learned to trust that even in the face of a total meltdown, you will be there without judgment.

PART VII
School Days

Navigating the
IEP Process

"True navigation begins in the human heart.
It's the most important map of all."

— *Elizabeth Kapu'uwailani Lindsey, explorer*

Chapter 22

What is an IEP, Anyway?

(And What's My Role as Parent?)

"In special education, there's too much
emphasis placed on the deficit and not
enough placed on the strength."

— *Temple Grandin, author, speaker, and professor with autism*

Time flies! Before long, your toddler becomes a preschooler, then a kindergartner, until suddenly they're graduating from high school. It is never too early nor too late to begin educational planning. From the age of 3 years, your child might be eligible for enrollment in a developmental preschool. Contact the special education department of your local school district or county office of education to determine how to access services. Here are some fast facts to get you started.

What is an IFSP?

- *The Individual Family Service Plan (IFSP)* was created by US Public Law 99-457 to provide special services for young children with developmental delays, from birth (or as soon as a delay is identified) until age three years.

- *IFSP services* are usually home-based. Therapists work with your child in a natural environment, most often the home.

- *IFSP services* are family-oriented, focusing on the needs of the child and the family to help enhance the child's development. Parental training is an important component.

What is an IEP?

- *The Individualized Education Program (IEP)* is defined in the Individuals with Disabilities Education Act (IDEA) as a written statement for every child with a disability between ages 3–22. It is developed, reviewed, and revised as needed in IEP meetings.

- *IEP services* are most often provided in a school setting, either in a mainstream environment along with typical peers, in a special education setting with peers with similar needs, or often a hybrid of the two.

- *The IEP* includes a description of a child's strengths and weaknesses, current functional levels, annual goals, and methods to achieve them, along with how progress toward those goals will be measured.

- *Unlike the IFSP,* which is focused on child and family needs at home, the IEP focuses on the student's academic and functional needs in school.

What paperwork do I need to keep?

- If you do not already have one, create a binder with a section for medical paperwork, such as immunization records and diagnostic reports, as well as a section for educational paperwork, such as report cards, school assessment reports, and IEPs.

- Keep a copy of every assessment report and IFSP or IEP meeting minutes you attend in your binder. Your school will give you a copy of each form after it has been signed.

Who decides on the goals my child should work on?

- The team works together to decide on appropriate goals. These should reflect the child's strengths, weaknesses, and current level of functioning.

- Teachers and therapists will develop ideas for goals they would like to include, and of course, your input is invaluable.

- Bring ideas of items you would like your child to work on to the meeting,

How often will I have these meetings?

- IFSP and IEP meetings are held at least annually, and the IFSP is reviewed at 6 months, which may or may not include a meeting.

- If established goals have been met, or if either the school or the parents see a need to meet between annual meetings, then more meetings are permissible.

What if I want to meet more often than once a year?

- It is your right to request an IEP or IFSP meeting when you see a need.

- Decide whether your concern requires a full IEP meeting or whether an informal meeting with your child's teacher or therapist will suffice.

- Once a request for an IEP meeting is made in writing, you should expect one to be scheduled within 30 days.

Do I need to prepare before my child's meeting?

- No specific preparation is required for parents, but you may wish to do some homework before the meeting. Go back to last year's IEP or IFSP and review the goals set at that time. How do you feel your child has done achieving those goals? Teachers and therapists will bring data documenting your child's progress, but if you have not noticed improvement, let them know.

- If you have been sent a notice of a meeting request, respond with your willingness to attend the meeting or whether you would like to reschedule.

- Complete the form and send it back as soon as possible so the team can plan accordingly.

- Remember that the school personnel are on your child's team and are your allies, not your adversaries.

What not to do at an IFSP or IEP meeting:

- Do not bring other children with you to the meeting, if possible. They will be bored and potentially disruptive. Your team could be distracted. If you need to meet at a different time to allow for childcare, ask your IEP team for allowances.

- Do not take your frustrations out on the teacher if your child is not making the progress you hoped for. Do not yell or berate team members, even if you feel they have not done all that is needed. You will catch more flies with honey than with vinegar.

- Do not threaten to sue if you do not like their attitudes or disagree with their assessments of your child's abilities. If there are serious, legal issues which you have tried unsuccessfully to resolve, and you believe that your school refuses to comply with their legal obligations, you have the right to file a complaint with the state department of education. You may also get the services of a special need's advocate to ensure your child's rights are being protected.

What to do at an IFSP or IEP meeting:

- Arrive on time and be prepared with your binder and ideas for goals.

- Remember that each child learns at their own pace and in their own time.

- Pay attention to the strengths that the team reports. Share your own thoughts on your child's strengths and interests.

- Remain optimistic about your child's deficits. Everyone has weaknesses, and this team is committed to helping your child build on strengths to improve areas of need.

- Ask questions when you do not understand.

- Thank your child's team for their care and the work they undertake on your child's behalf.

Your child's educational team will join you in making your child's progress a priority. Be their ally, supporting them as they support your child. The annual educational meetings provide a written paper trail of your child's path toward adulthood, so you can look back and see how far they have come. Use it as a celebration of strengths and of their continuing development.

Chapter 23

Transition: Vocational

"Children with ASD often have many strengths that
would be valuable in the workplace."

— *~ Lisa Tew and Diane Zajac, authors* Autism and Employment:
Raising Your Child with Foundational Skills for The Future

Any parent knows their child's wonderful strengths, even if there are also challenges to be faced. Who among us does not have personal weaknesses in addition to strong points? Strive to identify your child's skills and interests, and encourage them to explore and dive into their passions. Who knows? Today's special interest may lead to tomorrow's employment opportunities.

When should I start thinking about my child's future employment?

- *It is never too soon.* You can start working on the prerequisite skills your child will need in the job market right away, beginning with the end in mind. At school, encourage your preschooler to bring a toy for sharing time and say something about it. Older children can give oral book reports or share a current event with the class. At home, have them talk about their day or tell a story at the dinner table, just as the siblings can. Let them practice each of these ahead of time to give them confidence. Do you want your adult child to be confident in a job interview? Give your young child opportunities to talk in front of others!

- *It is never too late.* Perhaps your child is older, and you come to recognize they might struggle with employment as an adult. It is easy to believe that a child who performs well on an IQ test, for example, will easily matriculate from high school to college to a career on their own. Unfortunately, this is not always the case with children with ASD. Even those called "high-functioning" or "low support needs" individuals are too often unemployed or under-employed in adulthood. Now that you realize your older child or teen may need help, you can start by working on the skills they will need. Begin where they are and proceed.

What skills will my child need to be employable in the future?

- *Communication Skills.* Communication is a core disability associated with ASD. Address all aspects of communication, including receptive (listening, reading) as well as expressive (speaking, writing.) If your child does not speak comfortably but does type, encourage them to express themselves in writing. Much communication in the workplace is done by email, and mastering this skill will be invaluable.

- *People Skills.* Social interaction is a core challenge your child will likely struggle with. Encourage them to work cooperatively with others, whether on school group assignments or chores at home that might require teamwork with siblings. Prepping and cooking a meal, setting the table, and cleaning up afterward are activities which lend themselves to teamwork practice.

- **Coping Skills.** Emotional self-regulation, flexibility, turn-taking, delaying gratification, and moving on to something new when faced with change are important coping skills. A young child can learn these skills playing games with the family. Do not always permit your child to go first or have their first choice of game token, and do not let them win by cheating in their favor. They will not learn to lose graciously with others if they have never experienced it at home in a safe environment. A young child who is allowed to blow out the candles and open the presents at every other family member's birthday party will not be liked when invited to a friend's party. Grandma may be happy to let her precious grandchild help her with the candles and unwrapping, but she does the child a disservice. Everyone must learn that sometimes, someone else gets to be the star in the spotlight. If they do learn this lesson early, they will be invited a second time to parties with peers. Expand this idea to the workplace: no one wants to work with someone who believes the world revolves around them. Learning to cope with small disappointments as a child rather than being shielded and spoiled will help them cope with the reality of adult life.

What do employers want?

- **Productive workers.** Bosses want workers who do the job and do not slack off. Employers will want to hire someone with skills to do the job and the work ethic to keep doing it even when they do not feel like it. Work ethic can be encouraged early by reinforcing working hard on school tasks or chores. Praise them specifically for how hard they worked. For example, "I like how you kept trying on that problem until you got it" or "It makes me feel good to see you sticking with your chore list until you were finished. That helps our family!"

- **_Team players._** Bosses want workers who get along with others. If someone is always complaining or being complained about for whatever reason, they are more likely to be passed over for promotion, or even let go when the company is laying off workers. This is an area of challenge for many people with ASD. If your child has an extreme response to seeing someone breaking a rule, such as crossing a street in the middle of the block, they are likely to be the one who notices all their colleagues' minor infractions. No one likes working with someone who points out who took an extra break or posted on social media when they should have been working or made a private phone call on company time. From early on, teach your child the difference between an emergency (a child fell off the slide and is bleeding profusely or unconscious: we should call 911) and a non-emergency (a child went up the slide instead of up the ladder: we should mind our own business). Another challenge to being a good team player is trying to do an entire project alone and ignoring the input of team members—or avoiding the group project altogether because collaboration is stressful. In school and at home, encourage cooperating on group projects or tasks and accepting the input of others. That can be easily modeled during family activities.

What barriers could get in the way?

- *The job interview.* This is perhaps the most difficult barrier to getting a job. Many adults with autism find that even though they might have exceptional skills, education, and ability to do a job effectively, jobs are given to people who are better at talking about the job during the interview. Watch videos of job interviews and participate in mock interviews. That is pre-learning—and Social Stories can be used here as well. The earlier one starts and the more practice one gets at interviewing, the more comfortable the process will be. Young children can "interview" for the chores they would most like to do. Ask them what experience they have had with this chore, what their strengths are, what weaknesses might get in the way of their ability to complete the job, and what they might do to ensure the job gets done despite the weakness. For example, when applying for the job of feeding the family dog:

Experience: "I fed the dog once when Mom asked for help."
Strength: "I love the dog."
Weakness: "I don't like the smell of the dog food."
What to do about that: "I can wear a face mask with a drop of vanilla on it to help with the dog food smell."

- *The "likability" issue.* Sadly, sometimes other people do not like children with ASD. Some adults strive to mask their autistic characteristics and can come on too strong. Others tell people up front about their autism, to mixed reviews. Some, when told a colleague is autistic, take the information in stride. Others may believe myths or misinformation about autism and form a negative view. Still others may not believe they have autism because they have masked so successfully; they think the person is just making excuses or trying to get out of work. These responses do not lend themselves to likability. However, if you begin social skills training early by teaching a child to be a good friend and a good listener, it can go a long way to improving future likability.

How can I help my child overcome the barriers to employment?

- **Work on foundational skills.** Communication, social skills, perspective taking, flexibility, respect, problem-solving, conflict negotiation, emotional intelligence, self-management skills, and the ability to self-soothe and self-regulate are all important foundational skills.

- **Work with a mentor.** When your child is old enough for an internship, apprenticeship, or entry-level work opportunities, seek out someone in their field of interest who might be willing to be a mentor to them. This might be a friend of the family or someone from school, your religious community, or a mentorship program. Having a person to look up to for guidance is a valuable rung on the ladder for successful future employment.

- **Work around the system.** Within ethical limits, pull any strings you can to get your child's foot in the door, even possibly bypassing the interview process. Dr. Temple Grandin, author, speaker, and expert in her field, never got a job by interviewing for it. She had exceptional skills, an impressive portfolio, and supporters on her side. Her talent spoke for itself in ways that she might not have been able to do during an interview. Help your child put together a portfolio of their strengths, experiences, and expertise. It will say more than a thousand words!

The path to future employment may not run straight and clear with no hurdles to leap. But there is a path. Do not cling to any pre-set idea of what you believe your child should become; remember, this is their future, not yours, and they must pursue their own dreams. As parents, we may feel that our child who loves animals and has strong academic skills would make a wonderful veterinarian. However, if that child finds the sight of blood nauseating, or if they become emotionally invested in every animal so that illness and death are deeply disturbing to them, this is not their path. Perhaps they will find joy in being a dog groomer. Perhaps they will choose a career unrelated to animals and channel their passion into pet ownership. Maybe they will volunteer at a no-kill animal shelter. Ultimately, they are the ones to determine how they want to live their lives. Our role is to nurture interests, teach skills, encourage experiences, and love unconditionally.

PART VIII
Transitions

Look the Future in the Eye Without Blinking

"Our anxiety does not come from thinking about
the future, but from wanting to control it."
— *Kahlil Gibran*

"The best thing about the future is that it
comes one day at a time."
— *Abraham Lincoln*

Chapter 24

Pre-Adolescence and the Dreaded Teen Years

"We cannot always build the future for our youth,
but we can build our youth for the future."

— *Franklin Delano Roosevelt*

Teen years are challenging for any parent—and for every child. The tornado of new emotions, social expectations, hormones, and changing life roles occurs all at once. For children with ASD who do not do well with change, these years are even more difficult. We need to prepare our children to enter the adult world with the tools necessary to succeed.

Is parenting a teenager as terrible as everyone says?

- **Yes.** The challenge of parenting a teen, with or without ASD, is formidable. Most parents experience major stress during these teen years.

- **But also no.** Your child at 16 and at 26 is the same child you adored at 6 weeks and 6, despite the whirlwind of changes. Parenting teens can be immensely rewarding and exciting. It is fun considering who is raising whom!

Should I pull back and be less involved now, so my teen can be independent?

- **Yes.** It is vital to allow your child to do more for themselves. This is especially true with self-care. If you have been bathing and shampooing your child until now, it is high time they attempt to learn to do this independently. Visual schedules of steps to take are useful and readily available online. (This is not just lather, rinse, repeat, but also put the lid back on the shampoo bottle and notify an adult when you run out of shampoo.)

- **But also no.** The teen years are not the time to pull back as if your parenting job is through. You are not finished. Although you will gradually allow your child the space to perform tasks independently, teens need to know that their parents are still there for them. They may need to talk, or they may just need to know that you continue to be their safe home base, always on their side.

Should I encourage age appropriate interests and activities even if my child is delayed?

- **Yes.** Absolutely. Even if they appear young in style and still adore the cartoons they watched as a child, they may also become interested in typical teen activities. It may be these new interests reflect a strong desire to fit in with peers, which every teen feels, or that their interests are changing naturally, as they do. In any case, your acceptance and encouragement mean a lot to them, whether or not they show it.

- *But also no.* Do not try to steer your child toward "age-appropriate" interests or actively discourage the interests they have had since childhood. Many adults still love Legos and cartoons. And what is so wrong with that?

Should I bring up sex education?

- *Yes.* Even if your child appears immature socially and naïve, their bodies are going through hormonal changes, and they need to know about it. Peers in school will be talking about sex, too, whether you like it or not. Make sure your child appreciates your values regarding sex, so that locker room talk is not the only side they know.

- *And yet...* Do not offer too much information too soon. At age 11 or 12, they may need to know the basics of how their bodies are being affected and where babies come from, but that may be enough.

- *Think before you dive in.* Whenever a child asks a question about sex, even if it appears to be inappropriate, stop yourself before blurting out answers or explanations. Rather, ask them. "Hmm, that's interesting. Why do you ask?" Seek to understand the context first. The explanations they are looking for are probably much simpler than you think.

- *On the other hand,* do not delay too long to broach discussions regarding sexual activity, pregnancy, and the risks and responsibilities related to sex. By high school, children should be fully aware of sexual intercourse, especially the right to say no. Imagine a classmate saying they want to be your child's boyfriend or girlfriend, and that the typical thing boyfriends and girlfriends do is have sex. Without being aware of any alternative, they might believe they have no choice but to go along. Be sure they are armed with the information they need and a script to use if they are uncomfortable with a peer's suggestion.

How can I prepare my child for the future?

- *Training wheels.* Children need to know intuitively that you serve as their training wheels on the bicycle of life. Until they can do things on their own, you will be there to help them find balance when they wobble.

- *Band-Aids.* They also need to be assured that if they falter, you will help them recover, bandage that scraped knee, and help them get back on that bicycle. No matter the mistakes they make (and we all make mistakes), you will be there. You will always love them unconditionally, no matter what. No. Matter. What. Remember, there are no losers, "only winners and learners!" said Mandela.

Will we survive these years with our sanity intact?

- *Yes.* Parents have survived their children's teen years since the dawn of time and will continue to do so.

- *Just yes.* In the end, you will attain that future parents dream of, where your children are also your best friends. It is well worth waiting for.

- *And in the process,* our children will raise us!

Everything you have done for your child leads up to this: their graduation into adulthood. You started with the end in mind, and now you are nearing the goal. The key is planning for the unavoidable transitions. The next chapters address educational, financial, recreational, and vocational transitions.

Chapter 25

Transition Planning: Educational

"I might hit developmental and societal milestones in a different order than my peers, but I am able to accomplish these small victories on my own time."

— *Haley Moss, artist, author, attorney, and advocate with autism*

The educational system provides for transition planning through the IEP process. The term "transition services" refers to a coordinated, results-oriented set of activities designed to help children with disabilities prepare for life after high school. This may include college or other post-high school training programs, vocational education, supported employment, continuing and adult education, adult services, independent living, and community participation.

Transition plans are based on the student's unique needs along with personal strengths, preferences, interests, and the family culture.

Will my child have an educational transition plan?

- *Yes.* There is a legal requirement that the IEP team prepare an educational transition plan to facilitate moving from school to post-secondary activities.

When will the transition plan be written?

- *Before age 16.* At the IEP meeting covering the year in which your child turns 16, the team is required to prepare and include a transition plan. However, some schools begin even earlier, at age 13 or 14.

- *Ask* your child's IEP case manager when they expect to begin the transition process. The earlier the better!

Who will be on my child's transition planning team?

- *The IEP team.* This includes your child's teacher, who can also serve as the team's case manager, specialists they see in school, such as a behavioral therapist, SLP, OT, and a school administrator.

- *Of course,* it includes you and your child, as well as others you may invite. Throughout the IEP process, you as the parent have been the captain of your child's team. Now that your child is approaching adulthood, there will be a shift so that your child becomes more and more empowered to participate in their own education and transitional planning.

What happens once my child turns 18?

- *Congratulations! Your child becomes the adult.* On your child's 18th birthday, unless you have taken legal steps to become their guardian or conservator, your child becomes a legal adult with all the rights that bestows. You are no longer required to sign the IEP paperwork to approve the program, as your child will sign instead. If your child wants you at the meeting, you will sign in as an attendee, but now your child is in the driver's seat. Before then, the team will be wise to begin educating the student on the importance of the IEP process, along with its services and benefits. It can be disruptive to the learning process if a child decides to remove themselves from receiving special education services on their 18th birthday. Legal adults cannot be forced to accept services they decline.

What are guardianship and conservatorship?

- *Guardianship:* A guardian may be appointed for adults who have been deemed incapacitated or incompetent by a court of law and who will need substantial care throughout their lifetime. The guardian generally has legal authority to make personal and health-related decisions for people who cannot make these decisions for themselves.

- *Conservatorship:* The conservator has the legal authority to make financial decisions on behalf of individuals who are deemed unable to make such decisions for themselves—meaning they are completely unable to manage finances. Many young adults make foolish decisions with money, but they can learn from mistakes and continue to become more responsible. Having poor judgment is not necessarily incompetence.

- *Full adult rights:* In the absence of a court-appointed guardian and/or conservator, your child will have full adult rights at the age of 18. They may seek advice from you regarding important life decisions, as many young adults do, and it would be quite appropriate for you to continue to offer your support and guidance.

- **Seek legal advice** from a lawyer with extensive experience in disability law.

What is right for my child?

- **This is a personal decision.** It should be based on your child's current strengths and needs, and projecting what future level of service and support they might need.

- **Seek advice from experts.** Legal experts, educational experts, your adult's doctors, and others who know your child well can all provide input.

When should I make this decision?

- **Do not rush.** If your child is still young, do not worry yet. Continue intervening with the end in mind: your future independent adult child. Know there will be options available later when needed. Just because your child may not yet have daily living and functional communication skills, continued growth and development are to be expected. By adulthood, they may well have achieved many of the goals you had hoped for, even if reached on their own timelines.

- **Do not put if off until too late.** If by the teen years your child has not yet developed functional communication and self-care skills, and you realize they will need substantial support after their 18th birthday, do not delay until that month to begin the guardianship or conservatorship process. Bureaucratic wheels turn slowly. It will not happen overnight. Once your child is 18 years old with full rights, it may be a more difficult process. Seek legal guidance now!

Important decisions are made during the teen and transitional years. Continue to be an active participant on your child's IEP and Transition Planning team. Look at future options if post-high school needs are likely to require ongoing substantial support. Ask experts for help every step of the way. Remember, you began this process when first learning about autism with this end in mind: you are helping to facilitate and foster the independence of an adult ready to take their place in society as a productive citizen!

Chapter 26

Transition Planning: Financial

"Some of us are awesome at mathematics, and some of us struggle. That's okay because we're all different. But the most important part of mathematics is learning how to manage your money. Trust me, you'll need that skill when you're older."

— *Chris Bonello, teacher and author with autism*

Money does not buy happiness, to be sure, but the lack of money or ability to adequately manage money can buy unhappiness. Dr. Jed Baker wrote in his book, *Preparing for Life*, "Although there is more to life than money, having a comfortable amount of money can improve the quality of your life by allowing you to make more choices... The more money you have, the more freedom you have to choose what to do and where to live."

Parents naturally want their children to be financially savvy. Beginning with the end in mind, early childhood is a good place to start teaching about managing money.

Understanding money is more than knowing that ten pennies make a dime and 100 pennies make a dollar. We might assume that children who accompany us to the store every week would develop a basic awareness about making purchases. This is not always the case. So often, money is never actually seen during these exchanges—a plastic card is scanned or slid into a slot, buttons are pushed, and groceries are placed in bags.

Many children have very little concept about the family's finances. Some get frustrated when told there is not enough money to buy a desired toy. Clearly, in the child's view, all that is needed is to go to the magical ATM, and at the push of a few buttons, twenty-dollar bills slide out into your hand. They often fail to realize financial limitations.

So, how should parents help children better understand money?

Talk about it.

- *At home.* Before leaving to make a special purchase, discuss how much money you might expect the item to cost and how much money you are willing to pay.

- *In the store.* Talk about the prices of items you routinely buy, and point out the prices on the shelves. Briefly share your rationale for choosing an item based on a lower price or your willingness to pay a higher price for some items because of quality or preferences.

- *At the checkout line.* Narrate what you are doing. Tell your child that when you insert your card into the slot, the money is transferred from your bank account into the store's bank.

Role play with money.

- *Play store.* Use toy food and play money to make purchases.

- *Play restaurant.* Help your child design a menu for your pretend restaurant and decide how much money each item should cost. You can pretend to be a customer and order and pay for your toy food.

- *Make it real.* Perhaps your child wants to start a small in-home business, such as making cookies and lemonade. If they do the work, family members might pay a reasonable amount. Once a child is old enough to understand, they might even reimburse you for the ingredients!

Give an Allowance

- *Make it reasonable.* Exorbitant allowances are not beneficial. If needs and wants are easily met, they do not learn to work and save for a goal. This is important for your future adult child to know.

- *Make it meaningful.* If you go to the opposite extreme and pay your child only a few pennies for an allowance, they will not see it as meaningful. Make the objects of their desire attainable.

- *Make it regular.* Settle on an amount and a time to pay. Handing them whatever spare change you have whenever you happen to think of it is not an allowance, nor does it teach good money management. How would you feel if your employer were cavalier about when and how much you were paid? Whatever you decide about an allowance, follow through at regular times with the promised amount.

Require Chores

- *A family affair.* All households require upkeep. As a member of the family, give your child regular chores for which they are not paid. Pitching in and helping are family values and are performed without putting out a hand asking, "What will I get?" Beginning when they are quite young is the best way to start. Younger children can fold washcloths, match socks, or put away spoons from the dishwasher. As they grow, they can advance to putting away clean clothes and loading and unloading the dishwasher independently. You will get there, one baby step at a time.

- *To each their own.* Along with taking on family chores, children should be expected to take care of their own rooms. At first, supervise and cheer them on while they put their toys away into clearly marked bins. Organized storage makes the job easy. Later, they will be able to pick up their room on their own, dust, and even vacuum and change their own bedding.

Offer Jobs

- *Above and beyond.* In addition to their household chores and taking care of their own rooms, provide job opportunities to earn extra money. This might be when you need extra help, such as spring cleaning, or they may ask for a job when saving for something big.

- *But not too far out.* Your child may want $100 to buy a big-ticket item they have seen advertised on television. Do not be tempted to offer a large payout for minimal effort to help them reach their goal quickly. Giving a child $50 to sweep the front porch is not re-alistic. We know one boy who drew a picture and offered to sell it to his mother for $20 so he could buy a special toy. After negotia-tion, they settled on 25 cents. Children should learn the relative value of work to reward, and over-paying to satisfy their desires does not teach that lesson.

Spending Money

- **In person.** The next time you are in a store and are willing for your child to purchase a drink or a small toy, give them the actual mon-ey and let them buy it for themselves. The act of handing money to the cashier and receiving a purchase in return is meaningful.

- **Online.** Many purchases are made online. Once your child is old enough to read, teach them how you buy things online. Remind them of the relationship between pushing keys on a computer and your money leaving your account and going to the seller to pay for the item.

- **Do not share any passwords** that would allow your child to buy things without checking with you. Using your fingerprint as a passcode ensures that only you can spend your money. Supervise to stay internet-safe!

Saving Money

- **Short term.** Give your child opportunities to save for something they can afford if they save only a couple of allowances. This is a baby step between the immediate gratification of spending their whole allowance every time they get paid and the long-term goal of saving up their money to buy a big-ticket item.

- *Long term.* Eventually, you want your child to be able to manage money over a longer period. Planning to save a portion of each allowance is a good first step.

Borrowing Money

- *Loan.* Sometimes, a money-savvy child wants something that costs more than they have, such as a computer or phone. If it is something you agree is important to have sooner rather than waiting to save up for it, you may negotiate a loan with them. If you choose to charge interest, be sure they understand the concept, and make it reasonable. Put everything in writing, and each of you should sign it. If they fail to live up to their part of the bargain by making agreed-upon payments, put in the contract that you can temporarily re-possess the item until they get back on their payment plan. Being business-like now will help them in the future when they take out a loan for a car or house.

- *Credit.* Most people in our economy use credit. As your child grows older, make sure they understand the responsibilities and pitfalls of credit card ownership. It looks like free money. Paying it off is their future self's problem and not something their present self has to worry about. Many young people have fallen into credit card traps and end up paying exorbitant interest for years. Be straight with them about the dangers of accepting credit card offers that come in the mail or pop up online. If a deal looks too good to be true, beware.

Money management is a hallmark of adulthood. When your children are still young, get them started down the path of responsible earning, saving, and spending. These life lessons pay off in big dividends when your future adult child can balance a budget and take care of financial needs independently.

Chapter 27

Transition: Recreation

"Kids have to be exposed to different things in order to develop. A child's not going to find out he likes to play a musical instrument if you never exposed him to it."

— *Temple Grandin, author, speaker and professor with autism*

We all need recreational opportunities to promote happiness and keep our lives in balance. What kinds of activities should we provide for our children to help them learn to enjoy recreation as adults? We do not all march to the same beat of the drum, and what might be fun for one might not be another's cup of tea at all. Observe your child during expressions of pure joy. What seems to spark that joy? Nature? Technology? Repetitive movement? By allowing and providing the opportunities to experience the things your child loves, even if perceived as unusual to the rest of the world, you can help them refill their spiritual cup and balance the stresses of life with the beauty that is evident in the smallest of things.

What kinds of recreational activities should I introduce my child to?

- *Choose things you already know they like.* Have you ever seen your child spinning in circles in the backyard with a huge grin as they gaze up at the sky through the leaves of a tree? Going to a park to experience more trees or even riding a carousel might be a fun recreation activity. Is your child fascinated by examining very small things, such as grains of sand or rice or the tiniest toys? A magnifying glass might add to their experience, and when they are older, perhaps a microscope.

- *Try new things you think they might like.* If they have never tried or enjoyed team sports, but you know they love to run, cross country athletics may be a welcome recreational activity. It is often more satisfying to run in a straight line rather than to engage in socially competitive and possibly stressful team sports such as baseball. If they love water, moving to music, kicking, consider introducing swimming, dancing, or Taekwondo.

- *Avoid overly social or stressful activities.* If most of your child's peers play on a soccer league, but your child would prefer to watch the butterflies on the field rather than pay attention to the rules, do not sign them up for a team. Perhaps cousins in your family love to go fishing with Grandpa. If your child has a deep love of animals and finds this distressing, do not push them to join in. There will be other opportunities to have fun with cousins and grandparents.

What if my child does not want to do the recreational activities that I plan for them?

- *Do not stress.* Not everyone likes the same things, and that is just fine. Do not stick to the notion that they must finish everything they sign up for, or else they are "quitters." In life, we all must learn what we do and do not enjoy. Honor their preferences and allow them to gracefully bow out.

- *Do try something else.* Go back to what you know of your child. What gives them joy? What makes them laugh? Think of new activities that align with their interests or relate to their passions.

What if my child spends too much time alone in their room?

- *Allow them downtime and privacy.* How much time in their room is too much time? The answer may be quite different from what you expect. If children have been engaging in busy social activities, they might need a great deal of alone time to recharge their batteries. Sensory overload is another reason for retreating to the bedroom, where lights and sound can be controlled. In addition, if your child plays video games, they may win and feel good about themselves in the game, despite not feeling like a winner in the outside world. Life is hard, and video games can provide an escape, albeit a temporary one, from the stress of it all. This is not necessarily a bad thing.

- *Refrain from nagging.* If children feel badgered, they are more likely to want to remain in the safety of their rooms. If they request to eat their meals alone in their rooms, think about why this may be. When the family gathers around the dinner table, is there pressure to join conversations that may be challenging for your child to jump into? Is this a time when parents teach table manners so the child feels constantly corrected as they try to enjoy their meal? Many people with ASD have sensory triggers, which can make dinner time difficult to tolerate, such as the sound of chewing, the sound of utensils clanging against plates, or ice cubes clinking in glasses. There are other reasons a child might want to retreat. So, finding solutions to their individual issues is a better course of action than simply demanding compliance without understanding.

What if my child gets so involved in an activity that they do not want to stop?

- *Set a schedule.* Having a visual schedule at home, as they do at school, will show children that even though they must stop watching TV to do something else, there will be another opportunity for TV time later to look forward to. Be sure that the schedule includes activities the child enjoys, as well as the needed academic and developmental tasks that are required. If a child must transition from a highly preferred activity, such as a video game, to a disliked activity, such as picking up their room, insert a "medium-liked" activity in between. A child may strongly resist stopping the video game to pick up the room, but they may accept stopping the game to look at a book about a video game character. Once they have read the book for a while, it is easier to transition from the book to the chore.

- *Focus on the rule, not the activity.* One boy we knew loved dinosaurs. He loved them so much he wanted dinosaurs all the time, everywhere he went. He only wanted to read about, play with, and draw pictures of dinosaurs, dinosaurs, dinosaurs! When he became very excited with toy dinosaurs, making them roar and fight each other, the excitement sometimes escalated. He began chasing other children while extending his dinosaur toy at them and roaring. This was perceived as aggression. His mother wanted to eliminate all dinosaurs from his life, at school and home, to avoid "dinosaur-related aggression." As expected, this was devastating to the child, who mourned the loss of his dinosaurs. Possibly a better plan might have been to focus on the rule that was being broken: chasing children who do not want to be chased. This is against the rules, whether or not you are holding a dinosaur toy. The new plan was that if a dinosaur he was holding bothered other children, then that dinosaur was to be put on Time Out on a high shelf. At first, while he was adjusting to this, a different dinosaur would be given to him to hold. This was a chance to see if this other dinosaur could have good, quiet behavior. The boy could learn which behaviors were unacceptable and experience the consequences of breaking the rule—the aggressive dinosaur was removed— without losing his beloved dinosaurs completely or permanently.

When planning recreational activities, respect a child's interests and strengths. Follow their lead and be open to their communication, either spoken or behavioral, while offering new things to try that might be related to their passions. The rest of the family might also attempt joining in the activities the child with ASD enjoys. Even if it is as simple as turning around and watching the clouds and branches go by high above, if done as a family, it can lead to laughter and fun. Perhaps the family that spins together grins together!

PART IX
Parents & Children in the Time of COVID

"And let's end on the important note that vaccines are being developed by scientists, many of whom have autism. We need scientists with autism to end the pandemic."

— *Tony Attwood, Autism in Lockdown*

At the time of writing this book, we are coming to grips with the enormity of the psychosocial impact on those directly affected by COVID-19 as well as on the general population, both children and adults. This is especially true for children with ASD.

There are recommendations for keeping children safe and healthy. These not only are medically important, but also give children an opportunity to take control and cope with the situation. Remind them to wash their hands, use hand sanitizer, practice social distancing, and wear a mask outside the home.

Right now, anxiety commonly impacts children. Parents usually do a better job recognizing externalizing behaviors in their children, such as hyperactivity and acting out, rather than internalizing behaviors, such as anxiety and stress. Adults are more easily able to express feelings, whereas children are more likely to internalize their worries. You may see signs of it: your child may be cranky or clingy or have trouble sleeping. They may complain of stomachaches and headaches.

"Ever worry about stuff?" you may ask your child directly. You will often be amazed at the responses. Talking about feelings helps. Reassurance is one of the cornerstones of nurturing parenting. Remind children that doctors are learning as much as they can as quickly as they can about the virus and are taking steps to keep everyone safe.

Let your children know that you will do your best to make the world a safe place for them, that you will always be there for them. Maybe you can give them their own mantras or brief prayers to recite when stressed or nervous. It is surprising how many adults continue to use the words they learned from their loving parents in early childhood.

Reinforce that anxiety is normal and that lots of kids feel it. Reward brave, non-anxious behavior. Congratulate a child who says, "I wash my hands to stay safe!"

Provide children with tools for stress reduction. Teach the two basic steps to stress management. The first is to say, "I feel." We say that either out loud or using our inside voices. Say, "I feel ..." and then describe how we feel, like "I feel stressed," or "I feel worried." Sometimes, just saying "I feel ..." is enough to solve problems or at least diminish them.

The second step is to say how we can cope or what we can do. That is when we say, "I can ..." Here, we teach tools such as breath awareness, body awareness, and mind awareness to help children cope with stress and fears. This is outlined further in the chapter on negative feelings and anxiety management.

The "Stress Thermometer" in that chapter, which combines the "I feel" and "I can" tools, can be helpful. It allows children to grade or color-code the intensity of their feelings and come up with coping tools to address each level. Try using the "I feel" and the "I can" approach yourself in front of your children. You can model coping behaviors.

Keep young children away from frightening images on TV and social media. Discuss with older children what they are hearing on the news and correct any misinformation or rumors.

Use media for social connection. If kids are missing their friends, cousins, and grandparents, use creative apps such as playing UNO on Houseparty or connecting on Caribu.

Biorhythms are often lost at stressful times. Maintain routines for sleep and meals. Activities that enhance rhythmicity, such as playing music, swinging, and dancing, are calming.

- Try to have *breakfast together*.

- Decide *where* everyone will work most effectively and without distractions.

- Create a *daily schedule* that can hang where everyone can see it.

- List *times* for learning, exercise, meals, and especially afternoon breaks.

- *Include your own hours* as well, so children know when your workday is done.

- *Be creative* and prepare props and music, and dress up at dinner time!

- *Enjoy* playing games or watching a movie together in the evening.

- Stick with normal *bedtime routines*.

This is a time to emphasize emotional well-being above academic advancement. Be reassured; the kids will catch up. It is a time for parents to be kind to themselves and practice self-care. We need reminders to take breaks, practice mindfulness and stress management, and congratulate ourselves on a job well done.

In the future, children will look back and remember with awe how their parents coped!

"The future depends on what we do in the present."

— *Mahatma Gandhi*

POSTSCRIPT: Congratulations!

You are on the Right Track & Moving Forward ...

"Your child with autism has unlimited potential,
just like everyone else."

— *Temple Grandin, author, speaker, and professor with autism*

After reading this book, you may find yourself feeling just a bit overwhelmed. There is a lot to learn about parenting a child with ASD. Do not be discouraged. When the going gets tough, the tough get going. You can do this! By now you should understand that autism is not a parent's "fault."

Remember, in times of stress, to use your support system: your family members, friends, counselors, and your child's educational team. There are many programs, treatments, and services in place to help you along your journey. Taking advantage of them early on will make the road immeasurably smoother for you and your child, so congratulations, you have just taken the first step!

While there is no "cure" for autism, every child's skills and abilities, not to mention the quality and enjoyment of their lives, can be significantly improved. Each child is unique. Through trials, education, and experience, you will discover the treatments that fit your child best. Parents know their child better than anyone. You will discover what works. Above all, do not give up. If one approach does not work, try others—as many as it takes!

Thousands of doctors and researchers are working on ways to improve treatment. This is true in many areas, including social communication, behavior, sensory, motor, medical, nutrition, and psychology. Please join one of the many autism-focused support and advocacy groups—both local and national—that can keep you apprised of these advances. Local groups can lend much-needed practical and emotional support to parents by sharing information and personal experience.

The road is long, and of course there will be rough spots. But many have traversed this road, and the rewards are well worth the effort. Children with ASD make friends, develop academic skills, communicate, socialize, overcome behavior challenges, and do so much more. Adults with autism may earn college degrees and have fulfilling careers, marriages, and families of their own. Levels of achievement will vary, but our goal is to optimize the outcome of every individual and to make each child's life as rich and fulfilling as possible. By beginning with the end in mind, early intervention gives you and your child a head start, which makes this goal that much more attainable.

As you continue your journey, ask for help when needed. You will be modeling self-advocacy for your child; you want them to ask for help when they are in need. Take a break and rest to avoid being worn too thin. You will be modeling self-care for your child. This, too, is an important life lesson for coping with daily stressors.

Reach out to friends when you need people, and allow yourself the luxury of alone time when that is your desire. You will be modeling life balance for your child. Everyone deserves the right to choose when they want to be social and when they need to withdraw to recharge their batteries.

Be mindful of the many joys that are part of parenting this amazing, unique, little person in your life, and appreciate those little moments of wonder along the way. You will be modeling a mindful approach to life that will serve your child well in the future. Mindfulness may help your child learn to focus their attention on what is important, and it fosters acceptance and kindness.

Beginning with the end in mind, you pave the way for your child's journey through life. You cannot eliminate every hurdle they must cross, but you can prepare them to better cope with life's inevitable ups and downs. Return to this guide when new issues arise in your child's development, and read chapters anew as they relate to where you and your child are on the journey. Be confident in your commitment to their success in living their best life. Love them unconditionally. Give them training wheels when they need them, be ready with a hug when they fall, and help them get back on that bike as soon as they are ready.

You've got this!

"I wish you all success on your journey toward the future.
It is much brighter than you think!"
— *Dr. Raun Melmed*

RESOURCES

BOOKS:

American Psychiatric Association. (2013). *Diagnostic and Statistical Manual of Mental Disorders* (5ᵗʰ ed.).

Baker, J. (2005). *Preparing for Life: The Complete Guide for Transitioning to Adulthood for Those with Autism and Asperger's Syndrome.* Arlington, TX: Future Horizons, Inc.

Ball, J. and Brown-Lofland, K. (2020). *Autism After the Pandemic: A Step-by-Step Guide Back to School & Work.* Arlington, TX: Future Horizons, Inc.

Ball, J. (2019). *You Can't Make Me! Pro-Active Strategies for Positive Behavior Change in Children.* Arlington, TX: Future Horizons, Inc.

Bondy, A. and Frost, L. (2011). *A Picture's Worth: PECS and Other Visual Strategies in Autism.* Bethesda, MD: Woodbine House.

Future Horizons Authors. (2020). *Autism in Lockdown: Expert Tips and Insights on Coping with the COVID-19 Pandemic.* Arlington, TX: Future Horizons, Inc.

Grandin, T. and Barron, S. (2017). *Unwritten Rules of Social Relationships: Decoding Social Mysteries through the Unique Perspectives of Autism.* V. Zysk (Ed.). Arlington, TX: Future Horizons, Inc.

Higashida, N. (2015). *Fall Down 7 Times Get Up 8: A Young Man's Voice from the Silence of Autism.* New York, NY: Random House.

Higashida, N. (2015). *The Reason I Jump.* New York, NY: Random House.

Marsh, W. W. (2018). *The ABCs of Autism in the Classroom: Setting the Stage for Success.* Arlington, TX: Future Horizons, Inc.

Marsh, W. W., and Marsh, S. (2020). *Homeschooling, Autism Style: Reset for Success.* Arlington, TX: Future Horizons, Inc.

Marsh, W. W. (2020). *Independent Living with Autism: Your Roadmap to Success.* Arlington, TX: Future Horizons, Inc.

Melmed, R. D. (2007). *Autism Early Intervention Fast Facts: A Guide that Explains the Evaluations, Diagnoses, and Treatments for Children with Autism Spectrum Disorders.* Arlington, TX: Future Horizons, Inc.

Melmed, R. D., and Wheeler, M. (2015). *Autism and the Extended Family: A Guide for Those Outside the Immediate Family Who Know and Love Someone with Autism.* Arlington, TX: Future Horizons, Inc.

Melmed, R. D., with Sexton, A. (2016). *Marvin's Monster Diary: ADHD Attacks! (But I Rock It, Big Time) ST4 Mindfulness Book 1 for Kids.* Sanger, CA: Familius.

Melmed, R. D., with Sexton, A. (2017) *Timmy's Monster Diary: Screen Time Stress (But I Tame It, Big Time) ST4 Mindfulness Book 2 for Kids.* Sanger, CA: Familius.

Melmed, R. D., with Abramson, S.E. (2019) *Harriet's Monster Diary: Awfully Anxious (But I Squish it, Big Time) ST4 Mindfulness Book 3 for Kids*. Sanger, CA: Familius.

Melmed, R. D., with Larsen, C.B. (2019) *Marvin's Monster Diary, 2 (+ Lyssa!): ADHD Emotion Explosion (But I Triumph, Big Time) ST4 Mindfulness Book 4 for Kids*. Sanger, CA: Familius.

Melmed, R. D., with Larsen, C.B. (2020) *Marvin's Monster Diary, 3: Trouble with Friend (But I Get By, Big Time) ST4 Mindfulness Book 5 for Kids*. Sanger, CA: Familius.

Notbohm, E. (2019). *Ten Things Every Child With Autism Wishes You Knew*, third edition. Arlington, TX: Future Horizons, Inc.

Tew, L. and Zajac, D. (2018). *Autism and Employment: Raising Your Child with Foundational Skills for the Future*. Arlington, TX: Future Horizons, Inc.

Yacio, J. G. (2020). *COVID-19 Isn't Fair!* Arlington, TX: Future Horizons, Inc.

Yacio, J. G. (2015). *Temple Did It, and I Can, Too! Seven Simple Life Rules*. Arlington, TX: Future Horizons, Inc.

WEBSITES:

About autism:
https://www.autism-society.org/

About developmental milestones:
www.cdc.gov/ncbddd/actearly/milestones/milestones-2mo.html

About finding a lost child:

http://ridleyparkpolice.org/lost-child-safety-tips/

https://www.safewise.com/blog/what-to-do-when-your-child-goes-missing/

https://www.autismriskmanagement.com/dennis-debbaudt/

https://www.missingkids.org/

About Floortime:

https://www.stanleygreenspan.com/

About grocery shopping with kids:

https://www.webmd.com/parenting/features/grocery-shopping-kids#1

About hand sanitizer:

https://www.healthychildren.org/English/health-issues/conditions/COVID-19/Pages/Keep-Hand-Sanitizer-Out-of-Childrens-Reach.aspx

About hand-washing:

https://www.healthychildren.org/English/health-issues/conditions/prevention/Pages/Hand-Washing-A-Powerful-Antidote-to-Illness.aspx

About nutrition:

https://www.mayoclinic.org/healthy-lifestyle/childrens-health/in-depth/nutrition-for-kids/art-20049335

About Pandemic Social Stories:
www.carolgraysocialstories.com/pandemic-social-stories-direct-access/

About PECS:
https://pecsusa.com/pecs/

About RDI:
https://www.rdiconnect.com/about-rdi/

About social distancing:
https://www.healthychildren.org/English/health-issues/conditions/COVID-19/Pages/Social-Distancing-Why-Keeping-Your-Distance-Helps-Keep-Others-Safe.aspx

About Social Stories™:
https://carolgraysocialstories.com/

About special education regulations:
https://sites.ed.gov/idea/regs/b/d/300.320

About well-child check-ups:
www.healthline.com/find-care/articles/pediatricians/well-child-visits

www.mayoclinic.org/healthy-lifestyle/infant-and-toddler-health/in-depth/healthy-baby/art-20044767

VIDEOS:

About Autism:
https://www.youtube.com/user/neurowonderful

About COVID-19:
Cincinnati Children's Hospital Outreach
https://www.cincinnatichildrens.org/service/d/developmental-behavioral/patients/outreach
(Includes videos about wearing a mask, strategies to improve compliance and cooperation while homebound, behavior management basics, sleep hygiene tips, calming strategies in the COVID-19 storm, coping with disrupted routines, and continuing clinical care during social distancing and school/program closures.)

COVID-19 Video Teaching Story from the University of Miami and Nova Southeastern University Center for Autism and Related Disabilities (UM-NSU-CARD).
This is a helpful social narrative video to help individuals with autism understand the Coronavirus.
https://www.youtube.com/watch?v=xkZ23tDzN4c&feature=youtu.be

About Masks:
https://www.youtube.com/watch?v=QrbYXWkViO8

https://www.bing.com/videos/search?q=YouTube+TED-B+Wenn+Lawson&docid=608036299682744051&mid=-06376CA86D92A5478F8206376CA86D92A5478F82&view=detail&FORM=VIRE

PARENT COURSES:

UCONN: A free, web-based training program to educate caregivers in basic behavioral and naturalistic teaching principles. Must register. https://parenttraining.chip.uconn.edu/

Help is in Your Hands: 16 lessons with animated videos that walk caregivers through strategies to use with toddlers to support social communication. Must register. https://helpisinyourhands.org/course

ADEPT UC Davis Autism Distance Education Parent Training. A 10-lesson learning module which provides parents with tools to teach functional skills using applied behavior analysis. https://health.ucdavis.edu/mindinstitute/centers/cedd/adept.html

APPS:

Caribu:
https://caribu.com
Feeling connected to extended family while sheltering at home is important for children. This app allows families to connect through a video-call to read books, draw, and learn together in real-time no matter where they are. Free.

Exercise Buddy:
http://www.exercisebuddy.com/
Opportunities to facilitate physical activity during COVID-19 are critical. Exercise Buddy is an app which can help increase physical activity. One-time fee of $30.00 at this writing.

ARTICLES:

Bonello, Chris, "Fifty Pieces of Advice from an Autistic Man Written for Autistic Children." *Autistic Not Weird*, 9 Nov 2018. www.autisticnotweird.com/advice-for-children/

Hyman, S. L., Levy, S. E., & Meyers, S.M. (2020). Identification, evaluation, and management of children with Autism Spectrum Disorder. *Pediatrics*, 145 (1).

Moreno, M. A. (2018). How to Consider Screen Time Limits... for Parents. JAMA *Pediatrics*, 2018;172(1):104. Doi:10.1001'jamapediatrics.2-17.40401).

AUTISM TESTS:

Goldstein, S., & Naglieri, J.A. (2009). *Autism Spectrum Rating Scales (ASRS)*. Toronto, Ontario, Canada: Multi-Health Systems.

Le Couteur, A., Lord, C., & Rutter, M. (2000). *Autism Diagnostic Interview Revised (ADI-R)*. [Manual]. Torrance, CA: Western Psychological Services.

Lord, C., Luyster, R.J., Gotham, K., & Guthrie, W. (2012). *Autism Diagnostic Observation Schedule, Second Edition (ADOS-2)*. [Manual: Toddler Module]. Torrance, CA: Western Psychological Services.

Lord, C., Rutter, M., DiLavore, P.C., Risi, S., Gotham, K., & Bishop, S.L. (2012). *Autism Diagnostic Observation Schedule, Second Edition (ADOS-2)*. [Manual: Modules 1–4]. Torrance, CA: Western Psychological Services.

Monteiro, M.J., & Stegall, S. (2018). *Monteiro Interview Guidelines for Diagnosing the Autism Spectrum, Second Edition: A Sensory-Based Approach (MIGDAS-2)* [Manual]. Torrance, CA: Western Psychological Services.

Robins, D., Fein, D., & Barton, M. (2009). *Modified Checklist for Autism in Toddlers*, Revised (M-CHAT-R). https://m-chat.org/

Schopler, E., Van Bourgondien, M. E., Wellman, G. J., & Love, S. R. (2010). *Childhood Autism Rating Scale, Second Edition (CARS-2)* [Manual]. Torrance, CA: Western Psychological Services.

Squires, J., & Bricker, D. (2008). *Ages & Stages Questionnaire, Third Edition (ASQ-3)*. Baltimore, MD: Brookes Publishing.

ABOUT THE AUTHORS

Raun D. Melmed, MD, FAAP, developmental and behavioral pediatrician, is director of the Melmed Center in Scottsdale, Arizona, and co-founder and medical director of the Southwest Autism Research and Resource Center in Phoenix. He is an Associate Professor of Pediatrics at the University of Arizona and on faculty at Arizona State University. Dr. Melmed is an investigator of novel therapeutic agents in the treatment of autism, Fragile X, Angelman's disorder, and ADHD and on studies of tools used in the early diagnosis of developmental disorders.

He is the co-author of *Autism: Early Intervention*; *Autism and the Extended Family*; and *Autism in Lockdown,* and authored the *ST4 Mindfulness Book for Kids Series* including *Marvin's Monster Diary - ADHD Attacks, Timmy's Monster Diary: Screen Time Attacks!, Harriet's Monster Diary - Awfully Anxious, Marvin's Monster Diary 2 (+ Lyssa): ADHD Emotion Explosion (But I Triumph, Big Time)*, and *Marvin's Monster Diary 3: Trouble with Friends (But I Get By, Big Time!)* and soon to be released *Marvin's Monster Diary 4: Neighborhood Bully (But We Stand Up, Big Time).*

Wendela Whitcomb Marsh, MA, BCBA, RSD, is the author of *The ABCs of Autism in the Classroom: Setting the Stage for Success* and *Independent Living with Autism: Your Roadmap to Success.* She co-authored with her daughter, Siobhan Marsh, *Homeschooling, Autism Style: Reset for Success.* Dr. Marsh has been a special education teacher, school psychologist, autism assessment specialist, speaker, counselor, university instructor, and is a board-certified behavior analyst. She is the mother of two awesome individuals with autism and was married for twenty-seven years to an amazing man with Asperger's syndrome. People on the spectrum, and those who love and nurture them, are among her favorite people in the world. Dr. Marsh lives in Salem, Oregon with her three children and two cats.

Also by
Wendela Whitcomb Marsh

The **ABC**s of Autism in the Classroom

SETTING THE STAGE FOR SUCCESS

Marsh, MA, BCBA, RSD

Independent Living with Autism

Your Roadmap to Success

itcomb Marsh, BA, RSD

HOMESCHOOLING, AUTISM STYLE

RESET FOR SUCCESS

WENDELA WHITCOMB MARSH, MA, BCBA, RSD
with SIOBHAN MARSH

FUTURE HORIZONS INC.

Also by
Raun Melmed

Autism Early Intervention

FAST FACTS

A Guide That Explains the Evaluations, Diagnoses, and Treatments for Children with Autism Spectrum Disorders

Raun D. Melmed, MD

Autism
and the
Extended Family

A Guide for Those Outside the Immediate Family Who Know and Love Someone with Autism

Endorsed by Dr. Temple Grandin
Foreword by Eustacia Cutler, Temple's Mother

Raun Melmed, M.D. & Maria Wheeler, M.Ed.

(800) 489-0727
www.fhautism.com

CPSIA information can be obtained
at www.ICGtesting.com
Printed in the USA
LVHW020739040321
680525LV00005B/5